Life Beyond Life

SCRIPTURES AND MEDITATIONS ON THE AFTERLIFE

Robert Vroon

New Harbor Press
RAPID CITY, SD

Vroon/New Harbor Press
1601 Mt. Rushmore Rd, Ste 3288
Rapid City, SD 57701
www.NewHarborPress.com

Ordering Information:
Quantity sales. Special discounts are available on quantity purchases by corporations, associations, and others. For details, contact the "Special Sales Department" at the address above.

Life Beyond Life / Robert Vroon. —1st ed.
ISBN 978-1-63357-419-9

*Dedicated to my parents, Peter and Isabelle Vroon,
who faced death with a courage born of faith, and
are now with the Lord.*

Contents

ACKNOWLEDGEMENTS

I want to thank my wife, Beth, my partner in life and ministry, for her practical help and encouragement in this writing project.

I also want to thank Ron Jackson, Bob Koehler, Dale Jensen, and Jim Hoffner—as participants in my men's study group—who studied and discussed the first draft with me, and offered helpful feedback.

INTRODUCTION

As I begin to write this book, a pandemic is raging, and over 300,000 people have died of COVID-19 in the United States alone. (Before I finished writing the book, it was over 600,000.) People of all ages and conditions have been dying. A young member of our church told me of a thirty-one-year-old friend of his who died of it. But most of the people who are getting seriously ill and/or dying of COVID- 19 are over sixty-five and/or have underlying conditions.

Personally, I am over seventy, and have what would probably be considered an underlying condition.

During the pandemic, when much of my life has been shut down, I have had plenty of time to think about death. I suspect many people think about it, even in good times.

I think back to a few years ago when an older loved one shared these thoughts: "*As we get older, our bodies fall apart, and worse yet, our minds may fall apart. We experience pain and suffering, all kinds of losses, sickness, and death. Not much to look forward to, is it?*" No wonder so many older people suffer from depression! And, during the pandemic, even middle-aged and younger persons have struggled with it.

Though I am now officially retired, I spent over thirty-five years in full-time pastoral ministry. My best estimate is that I officiated at more than 100 funerals during those years. Some of those were young people, but most were older. None of them were easy. The pain of separation from a loved one was usually intense. I always felt like weeping but, as the pastor, I felt that I was the one who had had to "keep it together."

In some ways, I felt helpless at funerals. What people usually wanted was to bring their loved one back. Though I do believe in miracles, I have never been able to raise the dead! So, what could I offer to the grieving? Presence, love, and empathy. Helping people to celebrate the life of one they loved. And I could share the Christian hope through Scriptures and meditation.

So, why am I writing this book? First, I am writing it for me. I need to be reminded of the Christian hope. I need to get a comprehensive picture of the afterlife promised in Scripture.

Second, I am writing it out of pastoral concern for others who are facing their death or the death of their loved ones. I suspect that many Christians have no more than some vague idea of "going to heaven." It might help all of us to get the bigger picture of the Christian hope.

In my pastoral ministry, I sensed that there were two big questions people had. First, is there life after death? Second, is there life *before* death? In my ministry, I tended to focus more on the latter, except at funerals. But I have come to see that the two are very much related. If we do not understand and believe in the biblical answer to the first, we are less likely to ever find an answer to the second.

Now that I have spoken to the why of my writing, I want to address the how. I start with the assumption that the Bible is our authority. That impacts my methods, as I will explain later. At the same time, I have consulted creeds and theology books and commentaries to guide me in my interpretation of Scripture. I want to avoid viewpoints that contradict the understanding of the Church through the ages. I also want to avoid being narrowly sectarian. I have been a student of Christian spirituality of many church traditions, and I hope to maintain that perspective.

I also aim to avoid eschatological controversies, such as the details concerning the Millennium or the Rapture. I will stick to what is quite clear in Scripture and may thus de-emphasize topics that are open to widely divergent interpretations.

Each of six chapters is organized around a major theme. Key Scriptures are printed in the book, with the hope that the readers will read and study each passage for themselves, and then read the meditation I have written on that passage. You can think of the meditation as a mini sermon; the book may thus be seen as a devotional book.

What I write in the meditations is intended to be pastoral and spiritual. It is not intended to be a scholarly theological treatise or a commentary, though there may be some elements of each. My intended audience is laypeople, and I trust that a "pastor's heart" (guided by the Holy Spirit) has informed the content of the book.

The basic plan of the book needs some explaining. Given that the theme of the book is the afterlife, the first chapter (on death) may seem to be out of place. However, it provides essential background on the human problem for which the Christian hope is the solution. That problem is death—and all the other curses of sin in our world. Against the backdrop of the curse, God's solution and our hope make more sense. We can appreciate the good news more when it is seen in contrast to— and as an answer to—the bad news.

The next three chapters deal with the good news: resurrection, the new creation, and what happens to the departed before Jesus comes again. Then, in chapter 5, we explore the question of how this affects our life here and now. At the end of each of the first five chapters, there are study questions for each Bible passage. These are meant as an aid for group Bible study and may also be helpful for individual study.

The book will conclude with chapter 6, which summarizes the key themes in the previous chapters. This is a way of bringing it all together in one big picture. I have also included study questions at the end of this chapter.

Although the first chapter of the book may seem "heavy," I trust that by the end of the book, we will all come to see that "THE BEST IS YET TO COME!"

CHAPTER 1

DEATH: AN ENEMY AND A CURSE

Time, like an ever-rolling stream
Soon bears us all away.
We fly forgotten, as a dream
Dies at the opening day.

"O God Our Help in Ages Past" by Isaac Watts, 1719

1*Now the serpent was more crafty than any of the wild animals the LORD God had made. He said to the woman, "Did God really say, 'You must not eat from any tree in the garden'?"* 2 *The woman said to the serpent, "We may eat fruit from the trees in the garden,* 3 *but God did say, 'You must not eat fruit from the tree that is in the middle of the garden, and you must not touch it, or you will die.'"* 4 *"You will not certainly die," the serpent said to the woman.* 5 *"For God knows that when you eat from it your eyes will be opened, and you will be like God, knowing good and evil."* 6 *When the woman saw that the fruit of the tree was good for food and pleasing to the eye, and also desirable for gaining wisdom, she took some and ate it. She also gave* *some to her husband, who was with her, and he ate it.* 7 *Then the eyes of both of them were opened, and they realized they were naked; so they sewed fig leaves together and made coverings for themselves.* 8 *Then the man and his wife heard the sound of the LORD God as he was walking in the garden in the cool of the day, and they hid from the LORD God among the trees of the garden.*

16 *To the woman he said, "I will make your pains in childbearing very severe; with painful labor you will give birth to children. Your desire will be for your husband, and he will rule over you."* 17 *To Adam he said, "Because you listened to your wife and ate fruit from the tree about which I commanded you, 'You must not eat from it,' "Cursed is the ground because of you; through painful toil you will eat food from it all the days of your life.* 18 *It will produce thorns and thistles for you, and you will eat the plants of the field.* 19 *By the sweat of your brow you will eat your food until you return to the ground, since from it you were taken; for dust you are and to dust you will return."*

22 *And the LORD God said, "The man has now become like one of us, knowing good and evil. He must not be allowed to reach out his hand and take also from the tree of life and eat, and live forever."* 23 *So the LORD God banished him from the Garden of Eden to work the ground from which he had been taken.* 24 *After he drove the man out, he placed on the east side of the Garden of Eden cherubim and a flaming sword flashing back and forth to guard*

> *the way to the tree of life.* (Genesis 3:1–8, 16-19, 22–24 NIV)

This passage of Scripture is about how sin entered the world—and with it, death. Back in Genesis 2:17, God instructs Adam that he can eat of any tree in the garden except one—the tree of the knowledge of good and evil. If he eats of that, he will die.

Now we see his wife Eve being tempted (through a serpent) to do the very thing God said not to do. It starts with casting doubt on God's Word: *Did God really say that?* It moves on to questioning God's motives: *You really won't die, but instead will become like God. Hey, God is lying to you to keep you from something really good. He's holding out on you.* The final step in this progression is disobedience. She eats of the fruit and gives some to Adam.

In the next scene, Adam and Eve hide from God. They are probably feeling guilt and alienation from God. The wonderful relationship between them and God has been disrupted. This is the first— and perhaps the most significant—result of their disobedience.

Next God pronounces curses on the serpent, on Eve, and on Adam. These can be seen as divine punishment, or simply as a declaration of the natural consequences of their actions. Either way, it is clear that personal relationships, childbearing, and work will never be the same. Perhaps worst of all, God makes it clear that they will die. Death has now entered the world; all people and all creatures will be subject to it. From this point forward, life will not be what it was intended to be. From now on, all humans will be broken people living in a broken world.

Most of us are keenly aware that life is not what it was meant to be. And the problem goes right back to each one of us. We who were made in the image of God are now corrupted by the sin nature.

As Aleksandr Solzhenitsyn put it in *The Gulag Archipelago*, the line between good and evil runs through every human heart.

And what about death? Is it just a natural thing, like taking a nap? NO. Was it part of the good creation before sin entered the world? NO. The potential for death was there in chapter two of Genesis, and immortality was not guaranteed. The tree of life was in the garden, but after the fall into sin, humans were forcefully prevented from eating of it. As we read in Romans 5:12, "Sin entered the world through one man, and death through sin."

One more thing must be noted. The man and the woman were banished from the garden paradise. They could not in their own strength get back in. Part of what this implies is that they no longer had the same intimate relationship with God. That was now damaged. They had chosen to doubt God's goodness and love, and were now alienated from him. Since God is the source of life and of all goodness, that would have negative consequences.

In short, death is a curse, or as Paul puts it in I Corinthians 15:26, an enemy. Thus, "Man is destined to die once." (Hebrews 9:27) This may seem like nothing but bad news. But it is necessary to understand the problem, before we can appreciate the solution.

****

> 20 *For the creation was subjected to frustration, not by its own choice, but by the will of the one who subjected it, in hope* 21 *that the creation itself will be liberated from its bondage to decay and brought into the freedom and glory of the children of God.*

> 22 *We know that the whole creation has been groaning as in the pains of childbirth right up to the present time.* (Romans 8:20–22 NIV)

Nature can be beautiful. I love to take walks in our active senior community, where there are flowers in bloom—during all seasons. My wife and I love to take walks in beautiful forested areas, and along the beach overlooking the Pacific Ocean. In the warmer months, we sometimes go swimming in the ocean.

But, as delightful as nature can be, it can also be brutal. One of our daughters went swimming in that ocean, and got stung by a stingray. Her leg swelled up and became red and hot. She got a bad infection at the point of the sting and suffered pain and sickness for over a month.

Worse yet, a friend in one of the churches I pastored went swimming in the Atlantic Ocean near his vacation home. One day, a large wave picked him up and smashed him into the sand. His neck was broken, and he was killed instantly. All who loved him were devastated.

I remember reading a story in the news a few years ago, about a tornado that hit a town in the South. Everything it hit was reduced to rubble. Sadly, it did not miss the elementary school, while school was in session. Some of the children were killed. The parents interviewed by reporters were beside themselves with grief.

One last example is the COVID-19 epidemic that is going on as I write this. Over 500,000 have died in the last twelve months. Someone asked me recently if I know any people who have gotten this disease. Yes—a few dozen. A handful that I know of have died. Thus far, no one in my immediate family has contracted it. But everyone has been negatively impacted. There has been widespread economic pain, and significant psychological suffering in our church, in our nation, and in our world.

We are all suffering from what has been called "pandemic fatigue."

Yes, nature can be brutal. Why is that so? We have a hint in our previous passage where it speaks of thorns and thistles as a curse on nature because of sin entering the world. In our current passage, it speaks of creation being "subjected to frustration." Later, the passage notes that nature needs to be "liberated from its bondage to decay." And then it tells us that nature has been "groaning" under the curse. Not only do we as individuals need to be delivered from pain and suffering and death, the whole creation needs healing and redemption! What good would it do us to be redeemed if the whole world were still broken and full of tragedy? What we need is a community of renewed people living in a renewed earth. We will talk about that in future chapters. Hang in there—the good news is coming!

****

> 41 *Then a man named Jairus, a synagogue leader, came and fell at Jesus' feet, pleading with him to come to his house* 42 *because his only daughter, a girl of about twelve, was dying . . .* 49 *While Jesus was still speaking, someone came from the house of Jairus, the synagogue leader. "Your daughter is dead," he said. "Don't bother the teacher anymore."* 50 *Hearing this, Jesus said to Jairus, "Don't be afraid; just believe, and she will be healed."* 51 *When he arrived at the house of Jairus, he did not let anyone go in with him except Peter, John and James, and the child's father and mother.* 52 *Meanwhile, all the people were wailing and mourning for her. "Stop wailing," Jesus said. "She is not dead but asleep."* 53 *They laughed at him, knowing that she was dead.* 54 *But he took her by the hand*

> *and said, "My child, get up!"* 55 *Her spirit returned, and at once she stood up. Then Jesus told them to give her something to eat.* 56 *Her parents were astonished, but he ordered them not to tell anyone what had happened.* (Luke 8:41–24, 49–56 NIV)

This is a powerful passage, with many possible lessons in it. But, for our purpose in this book, we will focus on *bereavement*, the pain of being separated from a loved one. Jairus comes to Jesus and pleads with him to come heal his daughter. She was just twelve years old, she was his only daughter, and she was sick and dying. As a parent, I can really identify with Jairus pleading for the life of his daughter. Our children are not supposed to die before us, and as parents, we would do almost anything to prevent that. Losing a child must be one of the most painful things in life.

Losing any loved one is hard and causes great sorrow. It results in a painful separation. In my years of pastoral ministry, I officiated at over 100 funerals. At every one of them, the pain of separation was evident. There was much weeping, and many sad faces, much as in Luke 8.

In 1996, my mother died. My father did not want to live any longer, so he stopped taking treatments for his cancer. He died a year later. I felt deep sorrow for a long time, and it still comes back at times. In the first few years, how often did I pick up the phone to call them, only to remember that this was no longer possible? Though I was an adult, I felt like an orphan.

Jesus also experienced bereavement. Did you ever notice that his earthly father Joseph was last mentioned in a story about Jesus at the age of twelve? By the time Jesus starts his ministry at age thirty, Joseph is no longer on the scene. It is fair to assume that he has died. Somewhere between age twelve and age thirty, Jesus lost him. We may sometimes forget that Jesus was both God and man (see the Nicene Creed). As a human, he experienced the pain of bereavement.

In John 11:35, we are explicitly told that Jesus wept. The occasion was the death of his dear friend Lazarus. Even though he knew he was going to raise Lazarus from the dead, he wept as he himself felt the pain of bereavement and observed it in others. The curse of death takes a great toll on all of us, when we lose precious loved ones. And, if you live very long, you will experience it often. My mother used to say that one of the hardest things about growing old is that most of the people you have loved are dead.

In this passage and in John 11, something wonderful happens. Jesus raises the little girl from the dead—"Her spirit returned." And, in John 11, he raises Lazarus from the dead. If we think of the miracles of Jesus as signs pointing to the future Kingdom of God, these two miracles give us great hope for our future. So, in the midst of this chapter, which may seem a bit heavy, we have a hint of the good news to come.

But there is still one more passage on death to explore—one of many passages on the death of Jesus.

****

> 9 *But we do see Jesus, who was made lower than the angels for a little while, now crowned with glory and honor because he suffered death, so that by the grace of God he might taste death for everyone.* 10 *In bringing many sons and daughters to glory, it is fitting that God, for whom and through whom everything exists, should make the pioneer of their salvation perfect through what he suffered.* 11 *Both the one who makes people holy and those who are made holy are of the same family. So Jesus is not ashamed to call them brothers and sisters.* 12 *He*

> *says, "I will declare your name to my brothers and sisters; in the assembly I will sing your praises."* 13 *And again, "I will put my trust inhim." And again he says, "Here am I, and the children God has given me."* 14 *Since the children have flesh and blood, he too shared in their humanity so that by his death he might break the power of him who holds the power of death—that is, the devil—* 15 *and free those who all their lives were held in slavery by their fear of death.* 16 *For surely it is not angels he helps, but Abraham's descendants.* 17 *For this reason he had to be made like them, fully human in every way, in order that he might become a merciful and faithful high priest in service to God, and that he might make atonement for the sins of the people.* 18 *Because he himself suffered when he was tempted, he is able to help those who are being tempted.* (Hebrews 2:9–18 NIV)

This passage talks about the *Incarnation*, which means that the Son of God came to earth as a human being. As John 1:14 puts it, "The Word became flesh, and made his dwelling among us." Or, as in the current passage, "He had to be made like his brothers in every way." In other words, he had to be made like us, so he could experience human life much as we do. He had to experience the circumstances, the trials, the temptations, the sorrow, and the pain of human life. Why? So, he could be our sympathetic high priest, who intercedes for us with God the Father. And so could we know that he really loves us.

Most people in Jesus' day saw "the gods" as detached from human life. It was their prerogative to stay above the messy world we live in. Even the Jews believed that God would never condescend to subjecting himself to the mess of human life. But the God of the Bible decided to identify with us by sending his

Son to live among us as one of us. He decided to get in there and suffer with us. He decided to share in our humanity.

He had to deal with all the same things we have to deal with: hunger and thirst, cold and heat, tiredness, pain, temptations, and more. He had to deal with bereavement, as was mentioned earlier.

But most amazingly, he had to deal with his own death. We might think that God would have let his own Son dispense with that part of it. After all, death is the result of sin, and Jesus never committed any sin. So he should not have to die.

Of course, we are taught in many parts of the New Testament that Jesus died to *pay for* ("atone for") our sins, so we could be reconciled to God. But I also believe it was part of the Incarnation, part of his identifying with us. Death is part of the human experience—a part we would all like to avoid! Indeed, this passage speaks of us as "those who all their lives were held in slavery by their fear of death."

The Son of God surely had a right to skip this part of it, but he didn't. Think about it. He was arrested and charged with blasphemy against God, subversion of the Jewish faith, and treason/insurrection against the Roman Empire. He was not guilty of any of these things. But his trial was rigged. Those people on the Jewish high court (the *Sanhedrin*), who were sympathetic with Jesus, were conveniently not told about this trial. Then, the Roman governor, who knew Jesus was innocent, was politically pressured to sentence him to death.

Jesus had to die a very painful and humiliating death, with his enemies pouring out their hatred on him. Why did he have to go through all this? Jesus was identifying with us. Some of us have to deal with terrible injustices. All of us have to deal with some injustice—life is not fair! And many of us will have to die a painful death. It helps to know that God loved us so much, he got in there and suffered with us. Jesus understands us and is with us all the way.

STUDY GUIDE

GENESIS 3—SIN AND DEATH

1. In Genesis 2:16–17, what are God's instructions about eating the fruit of the tree?
2. What is the serpent's approach in trying to tempt Eve? Does it work?
3. What are the curses God places on Adam and Eve for their disobedience (in verses 16–19)?
4. What additional step does God take in verses 22–24?
5. Based on this passage, what would you say is the essence of the human problem?

ROMANS 8:20-22—NATURE IS BROKEN

1. What has creation been subjected to? (see verse 20)
2. Why is creation groaning? (see verse 22)
3. According to verse 21, what does creation need?
4. Has the curse of Genesis 3 extended to nature? Can you think of some examples of how nature is cursed or broken?

LUKE 41–42 and 49–56—BEREAVEMENT

1. What is the tone of Jairus' request for the healing of his daughter?
2. How are the people reacting to the young girl's death (in vs. 52)?
3. When have you experienced bereavement? How hard was it? Why?

HEBREWS 2:9–18—INCARNATION

1. What did it mean for the Son of God to become one of us? What did he experience?
2. According to verse 15, what are we enslaved by?
3. How did Jesus free us from this bondage?

4. How has knowing Jesus and his promises reduced your fear of death?

CHAPTER 2

RESURRECTION: HIS AND OURS

Soar we now where Christ has led, Alleluia!
Following our exalted Head. Alleluia! Made like
him, like him we rise, Alleluia
Ours the cross, the grave, the skies. Alleluia!

"Christ the Lord is Risen Today" by Charles Wesley

1On the first day of the week, very early in the morning, the women took the spices they had prepared and went to the tomb. 2 They found the stone rolled away from the tomb, 3 but when they entered, they did not find the body of the Lord Jesus. 4 While they were wondering about this, suddenly two men in clothes that gleamed like lightning stood beside them. 5 In their fright the women bowed down with their faces to the ground, but the men said to them, "Why do you look for the living among the dead? 6 He is not here; he has risen! Remember how he told you, while he was still with you in Galilee . . . 36 While they were still talking about this, Jesus himself stood among them and said to them, "Peace be with you." 37 They were startled and frightened,

> *thinking they saw a ghost.* 38 *He said to them, "Why are you troubled, and why do doubts rise in your minds?* 39 *Look at my hands and my feet. It is I myself! Touch me and see; a ghost does not have flesh and bones, as you see I have."*
>
> 40 *When he had said this, he showed them his hands and feet.* 41 *And while they still did not believe it because of joy and amazement, he asked them, "Do you have anything here to eat?"* 42 *They gave him a piece of broiled fish,* 43 *and he took it and ate it in their presence.* (Luke 24:1–6, 36–43 NIV)

It was Sunday morning, a group of women who were followers of Jesus went to the tomb where he was buried. Their intention was to embalm his body with burial spices. But the very large stone at the entrance of the tomb was rolled away, and the tomb was empty. They were wondering who took the body of Jesus (John 20:2). But then two angels appeared to them and announced: "He is not here; he has risen!" The women were clearly surprised. They were not expecting him to rise from the dead, or they would not have brought spices to embalm him. Yes, he had told them he would rise, but it apparently did not register. When they went back and told the eleven apostles, it "seemed to them like nonsense."

But later that day, Jesus appeared to the apostles in a room where the doors were closed and locked (see John 20:19). He didn't knock. He did not open the door. He came through the walls and appeared before them. Their reaction? They were startled and frightened. They were apparently not expecting him, and they thought they were seeing his ghost. Jesus invites them to look and see his hands and feet (which had been pierced by nails), and then invites them to touch him. And then he eats some food right before their eyes!

What kind of body could be touched, and eat food, and yet go through solid objects? It was a physical body, but one with very different physical properties. Theologians refer to it as Christ's "glorified body" after his resurrection.

I remember seeing an interview with a scientist, who was asked if it would be theoretically possible for a real physical body to go through walls or doors. He answered that if the molecules in the body were arranged differently, it would certainly be possible. Since none of us have ever seen such a body, it is understandable that we might find it difficult to believe it could exist. Hey, the disciples did not believe it at first, even though they saw it with their own eyes! That's because we tend to see what we expect to see. And our imagination may be limited to our relatively limited life experience. Being a fan of sci-fi, my imagination has been expanded. That makes it a little easier for me to believe the resurrection narratives. But, of course, in the end it comes down to faith in the Word of God.

A couple more things need to be said here about the resurrection of Jesus. First of all, there is a wonderful summary of Christ's resurrection appearances in verses 3–7 of 1 Corinthians 15. In addition to appearing to the apostles, he appeared to his brother James and, later, to a crowd of more than 500 believers, and finally to Paul on the road to Damascus. That's a lot of witnesses!

Second, if we look at the sermons of the apostles in the Book of Acts, we can see that the resurrection of Jesus was absolutely central to their faith and their preaching. Clearly this great truth was life-changing for them, and they were willing to risk their lives to spread the word.

> 17 *And if Christ has not been raised, your faith is futile; you are still in your sins.* 18 *Then those also*

> *who have fallen asleep in Christ are lost.* 19 *If only for this life we have hope in Christ, we are of all people most to be pitied.* 20 *But Christ has indeed been raised from the dead, the firstfruits of those who have fallen asleep.* 21 *For since death came through a man, the resurrection of the dead comes also through a man.* 22 *For as in Adam all die, so in Christ all will be made alive.* 23 *But each in turn: Christ, the firstfruits; then, when he comes, those who belong to him.* 24 *Then the end will come, when he hands over the kingdom to God the Father after he has destroyed all dominion, authority and power.* 25 *For he must reign until he has put all his enemies under his feet.* 26 *The last enemy to be destroyed is death . . .* 35 *But someone will ask, "How are the dead raised? With what kind of body will they come?"* 36 *How foolish! What you sow does not come to life unless it dies.* 37 *When you sow, you do not plant the body that will be, but just a seed, perhaps of wheat or of something else.* 38 *But God gives it a body as he has determined, and to each kind of seed he gives its own body . . .* 42 *So will it be with the resurrection of the dead. The body that is sown is perishable, it is raised imperishable;* 43 *it is sown in dishonor, it is raised in glory; it is sown in weakness, it is raised in power;* 44 *it is sown a natural body, it is raised a spiritual body. If there is a natural body, there is also a spiritual body.* (1 Corinthians 15:17–26, 35–38, 42–44 NIV)

First Corinthians chapter 15 is about resurrection—of Jesus and someday of us. Early in the chapter, Paul stresses the all-importance of Christ's resurrection. First, he says, if Christ has not been raised, we are still in our sins. There would be no atonement, because only the sinless Son of God could pay for our sins. But the proof of his being the Son of God (and the promised Messiah) **is** his resurrection. Without that, he is just a dead martyr. And we would still be lost.

Second, if Jesus has not been raised, our loved ones who have died are simply dead and gone forever. Because **our hope of an afterlife is based on the resurrection of Jesus**.

Paul goes on to say that if Christ is not risen, there is simply no hope in life. If death is the end of us, then even the present loses its meaning. Everything becomes hopeless and meaningless.

"But Christ has indeed been raised from the dead . . ." And that changes everything! Paul goes on to talk of Jesus as the "firstfruits." That is to say, he was the beginning of the harvest. He was the first person to rise from the dead, to a new body that can never die again. We who have trusted in him will be the rest of the harvest. But for us, that will happen when Jesus comes again. So, this is an unusual harvest in that the beginning of it precedes the rest of it by thousands of years.

But Paul makes it clear that our resurrection is inseparable from the resurrection of Jesus. They are two parts of one event. So, we might say that a piece of the resurrection of the saints at the end time has been split off and planted/inserted in the midst of history. Or, you might say that someone from another world has invaded our world! The resurrected Jesus is that someone. .He came from the world to come, and the age to come. He showed us our future and paved the way for it. Just as death came in into the world through Adam, so has resurrection come through Jesus the Messiah.

Then comes "the end," we are told. The Greek word translated as "the end" is a loaded word. It means the goal toward which the whole world is moving. That goal is the defeat and destruction of all that is evil in this world, including death itself.

Later in this passage, Paul poses the objections of the skeptics of his day. To the Greeks, the resurrection of the body seemed foolish. They were accustomed to Plato's idea that the body is a prison we should want to escape. So, they asked, how can this be? With what kind of body? How would this work? Perhaps what they are getting at is this question: *How can people rise when their bodies have disintegrated?*

Paul is not impressed with their lack of imagination. Literally, he says, "You, fools!" Look, we plant some withered-up, dried-out seeds in our garden, and beautiful plants grow up from them. And each seed produces its own kind of plant, with no two being exactly the same. Each seed is used by God to produce its own special body. When you think about it, this is strange. But we do not doubt it, because we have planted seeds, and seen the results. So why should we doubt such a transformation of the human body? Our body dies and is buried. But what will spring from it on the resurrection day is a body far more wonderful.

Our present body can and will die, but the new one cannot and will not die. The current one is sown in dishonor (sin), but the new one will be free of sin. Our body now has weaknesses and limitations, but the new one will be powerful. And it will be spiritual, though it will still be physical.

That's great, but will it be *me*? Yes. God gives to each seed its own body. So, in spite of the dissolution of the seed, and the change in its form, it's still the same life. There is continuity of identity. The seed has not lost its identity—it has simply blossomed into what it was ultimately intended to be. And so it will be with us: our bodies are dissolved by death, changed by resurrection, and yet it is still us who exist. We continue in a new form that is better suited for the new life. We are given a new body that is not subject to disease, decay, or death—and does not have all the limitations of our present body. But it is a physical body. Sin will be removed, and the image of God will be fully restored in us. Sounds good to me!

****

> 28 *"Do not be amazed at this, for a time is coming when all who are in their graves will hear his voice 29 and come out—those who have done what is good will rise to live, and those who have done what is evil will rise to be condemned.* (John 5:28–29 NIV)

> 24 *Martha answered, "I know he will rise again in the resurrection at the last day."* 25 *Jesus said to her, "I am the resurrection and the life. He who believes in me will live, even though he dies.* (John 11:24–25 NIV)

Who will be raised from the dead? All who have died: the good, the bad, the believers, the unbelievers. However, some will be raised to life, and others to condemnation. So, the day of resurrection will be good news for some, but bad news for others. Back in John 5:24, Jesus clarifies this. If we hear the word of Jesus, and put our faith in God the Father, we have passed over from death to life. When Jesus talks about "life" or "eternal life" in the Gospel of John, he is talking about life in fellowship with God. That is the life of the age to come, but it begins right here and now for those who believe in him.

What Jesus says in John 11:24–25 makes more sense in light of this. Martha has just affirmed her faith in the resurrection that is to occur at the end of time. She is affirming the Old Testament promise in Daniel 12:2—that those who sleep in the earth (the dead) will rise up, some to everlasting life, and others to shame and contempt.

Then, Jesus tells her that he is the one who has the power of resurrection in him. He is the life- giver. Those who believe in him, even if they die (physically), will continue to live in heaven and, later, in the new creation. And, in another sense, they will never die, which is to say that nothing (not even death) can interrupt their life in fellowship with God.

When Jesus speaks of faith in John, he literally invites us to "believe into him." That suggests more than mental assent to some teachings about him. It suggests entering into fellowship with him and walking with him in his way. It is a faith that includes *repentance*, which means a change of heart. We see that we have been walking in the wrong direction in life, so we make a decision to change directions. At that point, we have passed from death to life; the resurrection becomes a precious promise to us.

STUDY GUIDE

LUKE 24:1–6 AND 36–43—HIS RESURRECTION

1. Why were the women going to the tomb of Jesus? What did they find?
2. Who appears to the women? What do they say to them?
3. In verses 36–43, how did Jesus get into the room where the disciples were?
4. What did the disciples think they were seeing?
5. How does Jesus refute the disciples' fears?
6. Was his resurrection body a physical body? How different was his body? Is this a stretch for your imagination? Is it a stretch for your faith?

JOHN 5:28–29 AND JOHN 11:24–25—OUR RESURRECTION

1. According to John 5:28–29, who will be raised from the dead? Will this be a good thing for everyone?
2. In John 11, Jesus tells Martha that her brother will be raised from the dead. What is her response?
3. What does Jesus' response mean? (see verses 25–26)

1 CORINTHIANS 15—HOW HIS RESURRECTION AND OURS ARE CONNECTED

1. In verses 17–19, what would be the consequences if Jesus had not been raised? Why?
2. What is the meaning of *firstfruits*? How is Christ's resurrection the firstfruits of those who have died?
3. Who did death come from? How? Who does resurrection come from? How? When does our resurrection occur?
4. What does Paul mean by "the end" (verse 24)? What happens then?
5. What is the heart of the objection raised in verse 35? What is Paul's response?
6. Will we retain our individual identity? (see verse 38) Do all religions teach this? How satisfying would it be to just become a drop in the ocean of the great cosmic force?
7. How will our resurrection bodies be different from our present bodies? What four comparisons are made in verses 42–44? Is it still a physical body?

CHAPTER 3

THERE'S A NEW WORLD COMING!

The kingdom of this world
is become the kingdom of our Lord and of his Christ.
And he shall reign forever and ever . . .
King of kings and Lord of lords . . . Hallelujah!

"The Hallelujah Chorus" from *The Messiah*, by George Friedrich Handel

25 *"There will be signs in the sun, moon and stars. On the earth, nations will be in anguish and perplexity at the roaring and tossing of the sea.* 26 *People will faint from terror, apprehensive of what is coming on the world, for the heavenly bodies will be shaken.* 27 *At that time they will see the Son of Man coming in a cloud with power and great glory.* 28 *When these things begin to take place, stand up and lift up your heads, because your redemption is drawing near."* (Luke 21:25–28 NIV)

God has promised to remake or renew our world—and it all begins with the Second Coming of Christ. Our Lord talks about this in all three Synoptic Gospels. It will come at a very trying time on earth. Things will be going crazy in the sun, the moon, and the stars, and this will have a powerful effect on the seas. People will be full of fear over what is happening.

At that time Jesus will come in power and glory, and in a way that is very visible to everyone— no one alive at the time will miss it! Jesus then adds, "When you see all this, you will know that your redemption is drawing near." What does that mean? Part of what it means—as we read in 1 Corinthians 15—is the resurrection of the dead. As it is made clear in 1 Thessalonians 4:14–17, the dead in Christ will rise first to join with him in his coming. Then, those who are alive when Jesus comes will "meet the Lord in the air." That suggests they will not have to die, but will simply go straight to their resurrection bodies. "In a moment, in the twinkling of an eye . . . we shall be changed." (1 Corinthians 15:52). So, when Jesus says, "Our redemption is drawing near," he means the redemption of our bodies.

Jesus also means more than that. Our full redemption includes his victory over the powers of evil, the judgment of all people, and the bringing in of the new creation. These events are necessary to our redemption because the curse of sin goes beyond any individual. It pollutes every aspect of human life—our work, our relationships, our human institutions, our economic systems, and our political systems. Even if one person could personally be totally free of sin and its effects, his salvation would not be complete. She would have to relate to others who are sinful and be subject to systems that are polluted by evil. We need more than an individual solution. The whole human race and all of creation are polluted by evil and need to be cleaned up! This leads us into the passages that follow.

****

> 11 *I saw heaven standing open and there before me was a white horse, whose rider is called Faithful and True. With justice he judges and wages war.* 12 *His eyes are like blazing fire, and on his head are many crowns. He has a name written on him that no one knows but he himself.* 13 *He is dressed in a robe dipped in blood, and his name is the Word of God.* 14 *The armies of heaven were following him, riding on white horses and dressed in fine linen, white and clean.* 15 *Coming out of his mouth is a sharp sword with which to strike down the nations. "He will rule them with an iron scepter." He treads the winepress of the fury of the wrath of God Almighty.* 16 *On his robe and on his thigh he has this name written: KING OF KINGS AND LORD OF LORDS.* (Revelation 19:11–16 NIV)

This passage describes the Second Coming of Christ. In it, John emphasizes Christ's victory over the powers of evil. He is pictured on a white horse, a symbol of divine victory. He is called "faithful and true," because he can be depended on to bring about full salvation for his people.

Before he can accomplish this, he must rid the world of the evil powers which oppose him. It is important to see that he does not conquer his enemies in a vengeful or arbitrary spirit, but simply in accord with true justice. Notice that he fights them with the word of his mouth. This goes back to the creation story in Genesis. God created by his word. He said, "Let there be light, and there was light."

Here Jesus says in effect, let those who oppose God be defeated—and they are!

Christ's mission at his Second Coming is quite different from that of his first coming. The first time he came to seek and to save the lost. He willingly suffered at the hands of those who rejected him and his message. He revealed a God who wanted to win back lost sinners. But, when Jesus returns, he will come as a conqueror. He will visibly take the reins, and all will see that he is the King of Kings and Lord of Lords!

> **11** *Then I saw a great white throne and him who was seated on it. The earth and the heavens fled from his presence, and there was no place for them.* **12** *And I saw the dead, great and small, standing before the throne, and books were opened. Another book was opened, which is the book of life. The dead were judged according to what they had done as recorded in the books.* **13** *The sea gave up the dead that were in it, and death and Hades gave up the dead that were in them, and each person was judged according to what they had done.* **14** *Then death and Hades were thrown into the lake of fire. The lake of fire is the second death.* 15 *Anyone whose name was not found written in the book of life was thrown into the lake of fire.* (Revelation 20:11–15 NIV)

John sees God, seated on his throne. All people who have ever lived must stand before him to be judged. All of us will have to give an accounting to him for what we have done in our lives. One set of books is opened, which has the records of what we did in life. So, we all get to review both the right and wrong things we did: These things you did were good—for these reasons. These other things were bad. Yet others were mixed. It is important that we distinguish the good from the bad.

But once we have reviewed these things, it will become clear that none of us has been good enough to earn salvation. So, even though we are judged by what we have done, our *salvation* (or acquittal) is based on the contents of another book—the

Book of Life. If our names are written in the Book of Life, we are acquitted. If we have trusted in Jesus and his atoning death for our sins, we are counted as righteous. "For it is by grace you have been saved through faith—and this not from yourselves, it is the gift of God—not by works, so that no one can boast." (Ephesians 2:8–9) Otherwise, we would be condemned.

When I led a men's Bible study on this passage recently, they asked a good question: "If Christians are saved by grace through faith, why would God even bother to judge us by our deeds?" What's the point of reviewing our deeds if they are forgiven? This passage does not explain that. But I believe it could be explained this way: We need to see what we did wrong in our life. We need to acknowledge and renounce the evil in our life. We need to ask God to forgive us, and to remove the evil from us. This sets the table for the grace we receive because our name is written in the Book of Life.

Is it also possible that those who receive salvation will receive differing rewards, based on what they have done in life? There are some Scripture passages (like 1 Corinthians 3:10–15) that seem to suggest it. However, many passages suggest that the joy of all the redeemed will nevertheless be complete.

One more thing to note is that death and the grave are destroyed, banished from the new world God is about to create. I am reminded of 1 Corinthians 15:26, which tells us that, "The last enemy to be destroyed is death." What a relief that will be!

****

> 1 *Then I saw "a new heaven and a new earth," for the first heaven and the first earth had passed away, and there was no longer any sea.* 2 *I saw the Holy City, the new Jerusalem, coming down out of heaven from God, prepared as a bride beautifully dressed for her husband.* 3 *And I heard a loud voice*

> *from the throne saying, "Look! God's dwelling place is now among the people, and he will dwell with them. They will be his people, and God himself will be with them and be their God. 4 'He will wipe every tear from their eyes. There will be no more death or mourning or crying or pain, for the old order of things has passed away." 5 He who was seated on the throne said, "I am making everything new!" Then he said, "Write this down, for these words are trustworthy and true." 6 He said to me: "It is done. I am the Alpha and the Omega, the Beginning and the End. To the thirsty I will give water without cost from the spring of the water of life. 7 Those who are victorious will inherit all this, and I will be their God and they will be my children.*
> (Revelation 21:1–7 NIV)

Verse one speaks of a new heaven and a new earth. The ultimate destiny of God's people is on a new earth. We are not to spend eternity floating around as disembodied souls in a non-physical "heaven." The idea that salvation consists of escaping our physical bodies and a physical earth—that is simply not a biblical idea. It is rather an idea that comes from ancient Greek philosophers and has somehow slipped into Christian thinking through the years. Our destiny is to live in the new creation, with new resurrection bodies that are like that of Jesus after he rose from the dead, and which can never die. We will live on a redeemed earth. Our present universe will be transformed (or perhaps destroyed and remade from scratch) so that it can fulfill the purpose for which God originally created it. If the third chapter of Genesis can be entitled "Paradise Lost," Revelation 21 could be named "Paradise Restored." The new creation may resemble the perfect world of the Garden of Eden before the Fall.

Now, just think for a minute about all that is beautiful and good in this world of ours: blue skies, mountains, forests, the ocean, the beauty of spring, and so much more. Imagine a world in which all these things are preserved (or maybe even improved upon), but without all the bad things in our world. How does that new creation sound to you?

In the passage we see the "new Jerusalem coming down out of heaven from God." The Bible conceives of the heavenly Jerusalem (heaven) as the dwelling place of departed Christians between their death and resurrection (which place we will talk about more in the next chapter of this book). But notice that heaven is not their final destiny. The heavenly Jerusalem descends from heaven to take up its permanent location in the new creation. The inhabitants (being God's people throughout the ages) are described as a bride prepared for her husband (Jesus Christ).

Then, we see that God himself will be present with his people in this new world. Though we as Christians have the beginnings of restored fellowship with God here and now, it is incomplete and is apprehended only by faith, not by sight. But, in the new creation, it will be complete and perfect— direct and unmarred fellowship with the living God, who loves us with a perfect love. Wow! And faith will be replaced by sight, as chapter 22 indicates when it says that we will see God face to face. This uninhibited fellowship with our loving Father, in all his beauty and goodness, is truly THE HIGHLIGHT OF ALL THAT IS TO COME!

We will be able to walk and talk with God and get to know him more fully in a way we can only dream of now. And that's why we can truly say, "The best is yet to come!" This is the goal of all redemption. We were made for fellowship with God. We were made in love, by love, and for love.

The One who loves us will "wipe away all our tears." I think we can take that to mean depression will also flee. And pain and misery and death. Hey, let's not kid ourselves—life here and now is hard. At times, the sorrow and pain can seem overwhelming. But, in the new creation, all that misery will be gone. Indeed, sin will be gone. Death will be gone. No more funerals, bereavement, and mourning. No more separation from our Christian loved ones. Perfect joy and peace will reign supreme.

Why will that be so? Because the old order will pass away. God will make everything new! Not only that, but he will meet all our spiritual needs. Thirst in this and other passages represents a sense of spiritual need. We will be given to drink from the spring of the water of life, as we shall again see in chapter 22.

****

> *1 Then the angel showed me the river of the water of life, as clear as crystal, flowing from the throne of God and of the Lamb 2 down the middle of the great street of the city. On each side of the river stood the tree of life, bearing twelve crops of fruit, yielding its fruit every month. And the leaves of the tree are for the healing of the nations. 3 No longer will there be any curse. The throne of God and of the Lamb will be in the city, and his servants will serve him. 4 They will see his face, and his name will be on their foreheads. 5 There will be no more night. They will not need the light of a lamp or the light of the sun, for the Lord God will give them light. And they will reign for ever and ever.* (Revelation 22:1–5 NIV)

Here again we see this imagery of the river of the water of life, described as clear and pure, and flowing from the throne of God. It reminds me of John 4:10, where Jesus says he can give a person living water. And, in John 4:14, he says this water will well up to eternal life. The point is that God is the source of all life, and that life will be freely available to all in the new creation. Death will be gone, and life will reign supreme.

That river also waters the tree of life, which produces the fruit of eternal life, and has leaves that heal people. So there will be no sickness and no death in the new creation. The tree of life is an image drawn from Genesis 2:9. It was present in the Garden of Eden. But after Adam and Eve sinned, they were prevented from coming near this tree, lest they eat of its fruit and live forever (Genesis 3:22). But in the new earth, God's people can eat of it—all we want.

The results of sin have been reversed. That is clear when our passage says there will no longer be any curse—referring to the curse for sin in Genesis 3. It will be removed! And God will dwell with us.

Then, there is this little phrase, which it might be very easy to overlook: "His servants will serve him." Later, it adds, "They will reign forever . . ." This suggests that we will have work to do! Actually, this should not be surprising. There was work to do in the Garden of Eden before sin entered the world, which suggests that work was part of the good creation. It was a positive thing. But after the fall into sin, work becomes a "mixed bag." Frustration, pain, and weariness entered in. Bad bosses and nasty coworkers showed up. Our own sinful responses added to the woes.

When I first entered the secular workplace as a young person, I hoped for creative opportunities, collegiality in relationships, and self-fulfillment. Needless to say, I experienced much disillusionment. Many of my coworkers had become cynical and bitter. Later, when, with great idealism I went into pastoral ministry, I discovered that sin is present even in the church! The congregation's expectations did not always match God's directives, as found in Scripture. In many ways, the work was a great joy anyway. But it was also frustrating.

In the new creation—with sin no longer present to corrupt everything—the joy and fulfillment of work will be fully restored. Work will be a totally good thing. We are told in Exodus 20:11 that God worked. It is part of our being made in his image, that we need creative work to do.

N. T. Wright, in *Surprised by Hope*, has some great insights about work in the new creation: "There will be work to do and we shall relish doing it. All the skills and talents we have put to God's service in this present life—and perhaps too the interests and likings we gave up because they conflicted with our vocation—will be enhanced and ennobled and given back to us to be exercised to his glory." (161) This seems like good news to me. Sitting on a cloud playing a harp could quickly get so boring!

Something else that could joyfully occupy our time is hinted at where it says that we will see God's face. This suggests intimate fellowship with God. What a great privilege that will be! How exhilarating! Getting to know God could certainly take up much of our time and will surely lead to the worship described in passages such as Revelation 5:9–14.

I suspect we might also spend much time getting to know each other. And maybe exploring the universe? And so many other good and worthwhile pursuits we wish we had more time to do now!

****

> 9 *One of the seven angels who had the seven bowls full of the seven last plagues came and said to me, "Come, I will show you the bride, the wife of the Lamb."* 10 *And he carried me away in the Spirit to a mountain great and high, and showed me the Holy City, Jerusalem, coming down out of heaven from God.* 11 *It shone with the glory of God, and its brilliance was like that of a very precious jewel,*

> *like a jasper, clear as crystal.* 12 *It had a great, high wall with twelve gates, and with twelve angels at the gates. On the gates were written the names of the twelve tribes of Israel.* 13 *There were three gates on the east, three on the north, three on the south and three on the west.* 14 *The wall of the city had twelve foundations, and on them were the names of the twelve apostles of the Lamb.* 15 *The angel who talked with me had a measuring rod of gold to measure the city, its gates and its walls.* 16 *The city was laid out like a square, as long as it was wide. He measured the city with the rod and found it to be 12,000 stadia in length, and as wide and high as it is long.* 17 *The angel measured the wall using human measurement, and it was 144 cubits thick.* 18 *The wall was made of jasper, and the city of pure gold, as pure as glass.* 19 *The foundations of the city walls were decorated with every kind of precious stone. The first foundation was jasper, the second sapphire, the third agate, the fourth emerald,* 20 *the fifth onyx, the sixth ruby, the seventh chrysolite, the eighth beryl, the ninth topaz, the tenth turquoise, the eleventh jacinth, and the twelfth amethyst.* 21 *The twelve gates were twelve pearls, each gate made of a single pearl. The great street of the city was of gold, as pure as transparent glass.* (Revelation 21:9–21 NIV)

This passage describes the heavenly Jerusalem that has, by the time of the passage, come down out of heaven to the new earth. It shines with the glory of God. It is extravagant, glittering with precious jewels. It is breathtakingly beautiful. And it is large enough—1,400 miles long and 1,400 miles wide—to hold many people. God spares nothing in making this spectacular place! It makes a five-star hotel look cheap, and the Taj Mahal look less than spectacular!

The main thing I want to say about descriptions like this—and there are a number of them in the Book of Revelation—is that I believe we would do best to approach them as a right-brain exercise. In the Western world, we want to approach everything with our left brain (logically and with analysis), but I am convinced that some parts of Scripture appeal mainly to the right brain (imagination and intuition).

I would encourage the reader to take the time to *imagine* what this passage is trying to describe. Imagine it, feel it, experience it. I suspect that most of it is not meant to be taken literally, or to be analyzed. Instead, meditate on the overall picture that is being painted in words. Soak it in, enjoy it, appreciate it. Then rejoice in the Lord, who has prepared such a breathtakingly beautiful place for us— a place so wonderful that it is very hard to describe in any terms that we could easily understand.

STUDY GUIDE

LUKE 21:25–28

1. What will be happening in our world right before Jesus comes again?
2. What will be the reaction of people to the events on earth?
3. Who will see the Second Coming of Christ?
4. Jesus says, when we see these things, we will know our redemption is drawing near. What aspects of redemption might he be referring to? Do we need more than an individual redemption?

REVELATION 19:11–16

1. Who is this person described here, and what is he doing?
2. When do these events occur?

3. How is Christ's mission different at his Second Coming than it was at his first coming?

REVELATION 20:11–15

1. Who is the judge? Who has to stand before him?
2. On what basis are people judged? But what determines their eternal destiny? If salvation is by grace through faith, what is the point of judging believers by their deeds?
3. What happens to death and the grave?

REVELATION 21:1–7

1. What is our ultimate destiny as Christians? Where will we spend eternity? Where is God's dwelling place going to be?
2. What bad things will no longer exist?
3. What is the meaning of the water of life?

REVELATION 22:1–5

1. Where have we heard of the tree of life before? What does it bestow?
2. What does it mean that there will be no curse?
3. Will we have work to do in the new creation? What might it be?
4. What is implied when it says we will see God's face?

REVELATION 21:9–21

What is the new Jerusalem like? Take time to just imagine it. What are your general impressions? Does it sound like a great place to be?

CHAPTER 4

IN THE MEANTIME

Steal away, steal away, steal away to Jesus! Steal away steal away home, I ain't got long to stay here.
My Lord, he calls me, he calls me by the thunder;
The trumpet sounds within my soul; I ain't got long to stay here.

African-American spiritual

19 *"There was a rich man who was dressed in purple and fine linen and lived in luxury every day.* 20 *At his gate was laid a beggar named Lazarus, covered with sores* 21 *and longing to eat what fell from the rich man's table. Even the dogs came and licked his sores.* 22 *"The time came when the beggar died and the angels carried him to Abraham's side. The rich man also died and was buried.* 23 *In Hades, where he was in torment, he looked up and saw Abraham far away, with Lazarus by his side.* 24 *So he called to him, 'Father Abraham, have pity on me and send Lazarus to dip the tip of his finger in*

water and cool my tongue, because I am in agony in this fire.' 25 *"But Abraham replied, 'Son, remember that in your lifetime you received your good things, while Lazarus received bad things, but now he is comforted here and you are in agony.* 26 *And besides all this, between us and you a great chasm has been set in place, so that those who want to go from here to you cannot, nor can anyone cross over from there to us.'"* (Luke 16:19–26 NIV)

Jesus told this story to emphasize the importance of showing compassion to the needy and afflicted. Yet, in the process, he also indirectly affirmed some common beliefs about the afterlife among the Jews of his day. In other passages, he affirmed belief in the resurrection of the dead, which would happen on the "day of the Lord," which the New Testament also makes clear is the day of Christ's Second Coming. But, here in Luke 16, we have one of the few times Jesus speaks of what happens to believers who die before the Second Coming. This is what theologians refer to as "the intermediate state." The early church was not too concerned about this, because they expected the Second Coming in their lifetime. When it became clear that it could be a while before Jesus comes again, people started to talk about what might happen to departed believers in the meantime.

This passage—indeed the whole Bible—gives us a basic (but not very detailed) picture of the intermediate state. There are a few things that are quite clear. First, upon death the believer is escorted by the angels to a blessed place (heaven), here called "Abraham's side." Since Abraham is there, it seems likely that all of God's people are there. This suggests it would be a place where we are reunited with Christian loved ones who have died.

Second, it is to be noted that the people in both the blessed place and in hell are fully conscious. They are not sleeping, nor in some kind of dream state. They are aware of where they are and what is going on. Abraham also informs them that there is a chasm between heaven and hell, so that a person cannot go from one place to the other. Though the judgment day has not yet come, God knows where it is going for each person, and people have already been separated accordingly. Other passages of Scripture confirm these basic points, as we shall see.

****

> 39 *One of the criminals who hung there hurled insults at him: "Aren't you the Messiah? Save yourself and us!"* 40 *But the other criminal rebuked him. "Don't you fear God," he said, "since you are under the same sentence?* 41 *We are punished justly, for we are getting what our deeds deserve. But this man has done nothing wrong."* 42 *Then he said, "Jesus, remember me when you come into your kingdom.* 43 *Jesus answered him, "Truly I tell you, today you will be with me in paradise."* (Luke 23:39–43 NIV)

One of the persons being crucified alongside Jesus shows real faith in him when he says: "Remember me when you come into your kingdom." Since he is dying, it seems obvious that he is looking toward the next life. Jesus responds: "Today you will be with me in paradise." In that short statement, there are some great truths about the afterlife.

First of all, there is the word *today*. He does not say "on the day of resurrection" or "after a few days." He says "today." The point is that when we die, we go to this good place right away, even if our life before our conversion was not so good. This guy was a criminal—or perhaps a guerilla warrior or, you might even say, a terrorist. Any way you look at it, he probably did some very bad things in his day. But now he has come to faith in Christ, none too soon! Today . . . paradise.

The second great truth is, "You will be with me." The place we go to upon dying is a place where we will be with Jesus. When Christians talk about dying, they often say they are going to be with the Lord. Or, they say, my loved one went to be with the Lord. That in itself guarantees that it will be a wonderful place!

The third great truth in this statement is that we will be "in paradise." William Barclay, in his commentary on Luke, puts it this way: "The word *paradise* is a Persian word meaning a walled garden. When a Persian king wanted to do one of his subjects a very special honor, he made him a companion of the garden, which meant he was chosen to walk in the garden with the king."

This saying of Jesus may also be referring back to the Garden of Eden. Either way, the point is that when we die, we immediately go to a beautiful garden where we enjoy the companionship of God himself. In this blessed place, we joyfully wait for the day of the resurrection of our bodies when Jesus comes again.

****

> 1 *For we know that if the earthly tent we live in is destroyed, we have a building from God, an eternal house in heaven, not built by human hands.* 2 *Meanwhile we groan, longing to be clothed instead with our heavenly dwelling,* 3 *because when we are clothed, we will not be found naked.* 4 *For while we are in this tent, we groan and are burdened, because we do not wish to be unclothed but to be clothed instead with our heavenly dwelling, so that what is mortal may be swallowed up by life.* 5 *Now the one*

> *who has fashioned us for this very purpose is God, who has given us the Spirit as a deposit, guaranteeing what is to come. 6 Therefore we are always confident and know that as long as we are at home in the body we are away from the Lord. 7 For we live by faith, not by sight. 8 We are confident, I say, and would prefer to be away from the body and at home with the Lord.* (2 Corinthians 5:1–8 NIV)

In this passage, the apostle Paul compares our physical body to a tent. A tent is a temporary and flimsy dwelling. It's fine for camping out for a while, but most of us would prefer a more solid and long-lasting structure for the long run. Our present body is like a tent. It is temporary and vulnerable to disease, accidents, violence, and more. While we are in it, we have to deal with pain and sorrow and the effects of aging—and the uncomfortable prospect of imminent death.

So, Paul looks forward to our eternal house—to the glorified body we will receive when Jesus comes again (which we talked about in chapter 2). He does not want to simply shed his present body— he wants to receive that new one. But, until Jesus comes again, those who have died must live without a body. They are thus "naked."

But, should we feel sorry for our Christian loved ones who have died? Paul answers that question in verses 6–8. "Away from the body . . . at home with the Lord." That's the key. As long as we are in this body and on this earth, we must walk by faith, not by sight. We do not see God face to face. We can have some degree of fellowship with God, but not that greater face-to-face fellowship we can have in the afterlife.

That is why Paul makes it clear in verse 8 that he would prefer to go and be with the Lord, rather than stay in this life on earth. So, our departed Christian loved ones are better off than we are, and we will be better off when we join them.

Think of it this way. When we come to faith in Jesus, we begin to receive the down payment of our future inheritance—in this life! We experience a degree of fellowship with God and his people, a purpose for living, and the joy of the Lord. When we die, we move on to the next step. We receive the second installment. We experience more of our ultimate destiny. This life is more joyful and blessed than the first. But the ultimate joy and blessing await the Day of the Lord, when Jesus comes again.

****

> 9 *When he opened the fifth seal, I saw under the altar the souls of those who had been slain because of the word of God and the testimony they had maintained.* 10 *They called out in a loud voice, "How long, Sovereign Lord, holy and true, until you judge the inhabitants of the earth and avenge our blood?"* 11 *Then each of them was given a white robe, and they were told to wait a little longer, until the full number of their fellow servants, their brothers and sisters, were killed just as they had been.* (Revelation 6:9–11 NIV)

In this passage, the souls of departed Christians are pictured as being in a conscious state of blessedness, yet eagerly awaiting the resurrection of the body and the consummation of God's great redemptive plan. Those who were martyred for the faith long for God's judgment on those who wrongfully killed them. And all Christians long for the day when God will set things right!

NOTE: There are many details about the afterlife that are not clearly answered in Scripture. This is even more so in regard to the "intermediate state." I expected this chapter to be longer, but there is just limited biblical material on it. The details are simply not spelled out for us. That's where faith comes in. We can trust in God's goodness—he loves to bless his children. Rejoice in the overall picture we have been given, and trust God to fill in the details in a way that will meet our deepest needs.

STUDY GUIDE

LUKE 16:19–26

1. What happened to Lazarus when he dies? To the rich man?
2. Are the people (both in heaven and in hell) sleeping or fully conscious?
3. Why are they separated, even before the judgment day?

LUKE 23:39-43

1. How would you describe the second criminal? Is he aware of his sinfulness and his need for a savior? Does he show faith in Jesus? What does Jesus promise him?
2. What is paradise?
3. What else does Jesus tell us about this place in this passage? How great is that?
4. How soon after dying will the believer go there?

CORINTHIANS 5:1–8

1. To what does Paul compare our present body? Is a tent a good place to live long-term? What are the problems with our present body?
2. What does Paul long to be "clothed" in? How does he describe our condition till then?
3. Should we feel sorry for Christian loved ones who have died? Are they better off than we are?
4. Which would Paul prefer?
5. Though we do not know many details of the immediate afterlife, can we trust God to meet our deepest needs? Do

we know enough to look forward to it with joy? Can we be confident that something better lies ahead?

REVELATION 6:9–11

1. Who are these souls under the altar? Are they conscious or sleeping?
2. What are they crying out for? Why would they be eager for this?
3. What is the divine response to their cry?

CHAPTER 5

LIVING TODAY IN LIGHT OF THE FUTURE

We've a story to tell to the nations,
that shall turn their hearts to the right,
A story of truth and mercy
A story of peace and light.
For the darkness shall turn to dawning,
And the dawning to noonday bright,
And Christ's great kingdom shall come on earth,
The kingdom of love and light.

We've a Story to Tell to the Nations, by H. Earnest Nichol

We have talked about our future hope as Christians. But does this make a difference for our life here and now? How are we to respond to this hope? How are we to shape our values, perspective, and behaviors accordingly? I have identified six main answers to this question—again, with Scripture passages to meditate on.

1. Respond in faith to God's grace.

> **16** *For God so loved the world that he gave his one and only Son, that whoever believes in him shall not perish but have eternal life.* (John 3:16 NIV)

God gave us his Son, so whoever believes in him could have eternal life. The phrase *eternal life* (or sometimes simply "life") in the Gospel of John does not just suggest a life that lasts forever. It is a quality of life in fellowship with God that begins when we put our faith in Jesus and continues forever. Like salvation itself, we receive the beginnings of it now and the fullness of it in the next life.

What do we have to do to receive this life? We have to believe into Jesus. That's what the original Greek means. That suggests more than simply believing certain doctrines about Jesus. It implies entering into a relationship with him by faith.

> 14 *After John was put in prison, Jesus went into Galilee, proclaiming the good news of God.* 15 *"The time has come," he said. "The kingdom of God has come near. Repent and believe the good news!"* (Mark 1:14–15 NIV)

As Jesus began his public ministry, he preached the good news. And, in this passage, Mark gives us the basic content of his message. "The time has come"—the time of God's action to bring salvation to humanity. In Christ, God has invaded our world to bring in the Kingdom of God. In its beginnings, the Kingdom is the reign of God in the lives of those who receive it (and which will be brought to fullness in the afterlife).

What is our response to be? Repent and believe. The Greek word for *repent* literally means to change one's mind. We are called to have a new mindset toward God, toward Christ, toward ourselves, and toward life. The Hebrew word for it (which Mark surely has in mind) suggests a 180-degree turn. You are going down a road, and realize you are going in the wrong direction; so, you do an about-face and go the other way. That's the picture. It is a decision to turn around, because we realize we were going the wrong way.

"Faith" we have talked about above. But the point here is that repentance and believing go together—they are inseparable. The condition for salvation not a faith, which may or may not lead to repentance at some later time. Rather, it is *repentant faith*.

True faith always includes repentance.

> 8 *For it is by grace you have been saved, through faith—and this is not from yourselves, it is the gift of God—* 9 *not by works, so that no one can boast.* (Ephesians 2:8–9 NIV)

Lest we think we can earn salvation by good behavior, or by repentance, Paul reminds us here that salvation is by the grace of God. *Grace* means a gift that we do not deserve and cannot earn. God offers it to us out of the goodness of his heart. Repentant faith is the condition for receiving it, but is not a means of earning it. That is an important understanding this passage adds for us.

2. **Hope for the future replaces fear of death.**

> 14 *Since the children have flesh and blood, he too shared in their humanity so that by his death he might break the power of him who holds the power of death—that is, the devil—* 15 *and free those who all their lives were held in slavery by their fear of death.* (Hebrews 2:14–15 NIV)

This passage speaks of those who throughout their lives were enslaved by their fear of death. And it says that Jesus frees them from this fear. The natural response to thoughts of our death is fear. This is doubly true for people with no faith. Is it any surprise that many people try very hard to avoid thinking about death? During the current COVID-19 pandemic, it's a little harder to avoid thoughts about death.

And, yes, I think some people are "held in slavery by their fear of death." It seems to me that a life full of fear is really no life at all.

But look at the dramatic impact the resurrection had on Jesus' earliest disciples. When he was killed, they were despondent and hopeless and full of fear. But, when they came to see that he really was raised from the dead, they became joyful and courageous. Nothing could stop them from spreading the good news. Their life was no longer dominated by fear of death, because Jesus had conquered death! And he promised them, "Because I live, you also will live." (John 14:19)

For people who have no hope, all of life has the dust of death on it. But, for us who believe the Christian hope, everything has the dust of life on it. Our whole outlook is changed!

3. Is it all downhill from here, or is the best yet to come?

> 16 *Therefore we do not lose heart. Though outwardly we are wasting away, yet inwardly we are being renewed day by day.* 17 *For our light and momentary troubles are achieving for us an eternal glory that far outweighs them all.* 18 *So we fix our eyes not on what is seen, but on what is unseen, since what is seen is temporary, but what is unseen is eternal.* (2 Corinthians 4:16–18 NIV)

As we age, it is easy to conclude at some point that it's all downhill from here. We experience losses of all kinds. It may start out with, "I can't go jogging anymore because of my knees." Then, I find that I can't eat some of my favorite foods anymore. After a while, it may be that parts of our body that we used to take for granted just don't function well anymore. Then, some things may go wrong that are really life-threatening. Then, we find ourselves having to take several pills a day, if we can remember! So it would be easy to lose heart.

But Paul tells us that he and his coworkers do not lose heart. They know that their bodies are wasting away due to the wear and tear of life (and the beatings and their concerns for their converts and more). But inwardly they are being spiritually renewed day by day. And they know (verse 14) that God will raise them from the dead someday. So, they know that all their troubles they have to endure now are a small thing compared to the eternal glory they will someday be blessed with. They know THE BEST IS YET TO COME!

There is another (but similar) reason that older people may lose heart. They look at the world around them, and feel it is spiraling downward. "It just keeps getting worse, and there's no hope for it," they may say. Everything is just falling apart. The only hope is for Jesus to come again. Actually, they are right to see that there is no hope apart from God's intervention.

But it is easy for us to forget that God has intervened before by way of *revivals* (times of spiritual renewal). God can and does work through his people to bring real changes in our world. He used Christian abolitionists to help end slavery in many nations. He used Christians in South Africa to end apartheid through a mostly bloodless revolution, just when everyone thought there was no hope for that land. He used Christians within and outside the Soviet Union to bring down the tyranny of Soviet communism. He used Dr. Martin Luther King, Jr., to bring greater social justice for African Americans, and that was a Christian movement he led! I could go on. The point is that nothing is hopeless or irreversible where God is present.

So, do not lose heart. God is still at work in our world. And he has promised us that in the end, he will set all things right.

4. **Jesus is coming again, and we need to be ready!**

> 14 *"Again, it will be like a man going on a journey, who called his servants and entrusted his wealth to them.* 15 *To one he gave five bags of gold, to another two bags, and to another one bag, each according to his ability. Then he went on his journey.* 16 *The man who had received five bags of gold went at once and put his money to work and gained five bags more.* 17 *So also, the one with two bags of gold gained two more.* 18 *But the man who had received one bag went off, dug a hole in the ground and hid his master's money.* 19 *"After a long time the master of those servants returned and settled accounts with them.* 20 *The man who had received five bags of gold brought the other five. 'Master,' he said, 'you entrusted me with five bags of gold. See, I have gained five more.'*21 *"His master replied, 'Well done, good and faithful servant! You have been faithful with a few things; I will put you in charge of many things. Come and share your master's happiness!'* 22 *"The man with two bags of gold also came. 'Master,' he said, 'you entrusted me with two bags of gold; see, I have gained two more.'* 23 *"His master replied, 'Well done, good and faithful servant! You have been faithful with a few things; I will put you in charge of many things. Come and share your master's happiness!'*

> 24 *"Then the man who had received one bag of gold came. 'Master,' he said, 'I knew that you are a hard man, harvesting where you have not sown and gathering where you have not scattered seed.* 25 *So I was afraid and went out and hid your gold in the ground. See, here is what belongs to you.'* 26 *"His master replied, 'You wicked, lazy servant! So you knew that I harvest where I have not sown and gather where I have not scattered seed?* 27 *Well then, you should have put my money on deposit with the bankers, so that when I returned I would have received it back with interest.* 28 *"'So take the bag of gold from him and give it to the one who has ten bags.* 29 *For whoever has will be given more, and they will have an abundance. Whoever does not have, even what they have will be taken from them.* 30 *And throw that worthless servant outside, into the darkness, where there will be weeping and gnashing of teeth.'* (Matthew 25:14–30 NIV)

This is known as the Parable of the Talents. A *talent* was a large sum of money and, thus, stands for all the resources God has given us, with which we can advance the Kingdom of God. He gives different resources to different people, and he expects them to be faithful in using them. When the master returns, each of his servants is held accountable for what he has done with what he was given. That turns out well for the servants who invested what they were given for the Lord. But the servant who buried his talent did not do so well.

This parable was told in the context of teachings about the Second Coming. When Jesus comes again, we want to be found faithfully working at the ministries God has called us to do. We have been given spiritual gifts, natural abilities, money, and more. We need to invest them in the work of the Kingdom. Our contributions to the Kingdom will not be compared to those of Christians who are more gifted than we are. We just need to be found faithful.

****

> 31 "*When the Son of Man comes in his glory, and all the angels with him, he will sit on his glorious throne.* 32 *All the nations will be gathered before him, and he will separate the people one from another as a shepherd separates the sheep from the goats.* 33 *He will put the sheep on his right and the goats on his left.* 34 "*Then the King will say to those on his right, 'Come, you who are blessed by my Father; take your inheritance, the kingdom prepared for you since the creation of the world* 35 *For I was hungry and you gave me something to eat, I was thirsty and you gave me something to drink, I was a stranger and you invited me in,* 36 *I needed clothes and you clothed me, I was sick and you looked after me, I was in prison and you came to visit me.'* 37 "*Then the righteous will answer him, 'Lord, when did we see you hungry and feed you, or thirsty and give you something to drink?* 38 *When did we see you a stranger and invite you in, or needing clothes and clothe you?* 39 *When did we see you sick or in prison and go to visit you?'* 40 "*The King will reply, 'Truly I tell you, whatever you did for one of the least of these brothers and sisters of mine, you did for me.'* 41 "*Then he will say to those on his left, 'Depart from me, you who are cursed, into the eternal fire prepared for the devil and his angels.* 42 *For I was hungry and you gave me nothing to eat, I was thirsty and you gave me nothing to drink,*

> 43 *I was a stranger and you did not invite me in, I needed clothes and you did not clothe me, I was sick and in prison and you did not look after me.'* 44 *"They also will answer, 'Lord, when did we see you hungry or thirsty or a stranger or needing clothes or sick or in prison, and did not help you?'* 45 *"He will reply, 'Truly I tell you, whatever you did not do for one of the least of these, you did not do for me.'* 46 *"Then they will go away to eternal punishment, but the righteous to eternal life."* (Matthew 25:31–46 NIV)

Again, we have a parable told in the context of the Second Coming. Each person is held accountable for what they have done. In this case, the question is, "What have you done to help the needy and the hurting around you?" Did we help meet the basic needs (food and clothing) of the poor? Did we help the sick, and visit the prisoner? The Lord so identifies with such persons, that he sees our ministry to them as ministry to him.

If we have entered into a relationship with God through faith in Jesus, we will become more loving and compassionate toward the needy. We are called to continue the ministry of Jesus, and we will do so through both formal and informal ministries of mercy.

****

> 2 *Dear friends, now we are children of God, and what we will be has not yet been made known. But we know that when Christ appears, we shall be like him, for we shall see him as he is.* 3 *All who have this hope in him purify themselves, just as he is pure.* (1 John 3:2–3 NIV)

> 11 *Since everything will be destroyed in this way, what kind of people ought you to be? You ought to live holy and godly lives.* (2 Peter 3:11 NIV)

> 14 *And this gospel of the kingdom will be preached in the whole world as a testimony to all nations, and then the end will come.* (Matthew 24:14 NIV)

There are many theories and doctrines relating to the details of the end times and the Second Coming. Many of these are highly speculative, yet people will argue for their preferred viewpoints as if they were clear and basic Christian truth. I suspect that most of these Christian writers and teachers will someday (when they go to be with the Lord) discover that they were wrong on most of these issues. It may be better to stick to what is clear in Scripture and be very humble about what is not. "No one knows about that day or hour," Jesus says of his Second Coming. How much disillusionment and heartache could have been avoided in Christian history, if people had just taken that verse seriously!

Above all, we need to try not to get distracted by the unclear stuff, to the point that we miss what is really important. Virtually every New Testament passage on the Second Coming is directly linked with a call to godly living, faithful service, or spiritual growth. Let's be sure not to miss these spiritual applications to our lives. Let's be sure to be ready/prepared for his coming.

In 1 John 3, we are told that when Jesus appears, we shall be like him. So we need to *purify ourselves*—in other words, start becoming more like him now. In 2 Peter 3, we are told that we need to be leading holy and godly lives as we look forward to the day of his coming. In Matthew 24:14, we are called to preach the Gospel to all nations and, thus, hasten the day of his coming. In Luke 21:34, we are warned not to get weighed down with "dissipation, drunkenness, and the anxieties of life" as the day of his coming approaches.

The point is, as the day of the Lord approaches, we need to prepare for it by growing in Christian love and being faithful in Christian service. Don't get so caught up in speculative theologies that you miss these crucial life applications! The Second Coming has major implications for how we live our lives now.

5. **Pictures of the future Kingdom of God help us know what to aim for, as we seek to bring in the beginnings of the Kingdom now.**

> ***1*** *A shoot will come up from the stump of Jesse; from his roots a Branch will bear fruit.* ***2*** *The Spirit of the LORD will rest on him— the Spirit of wisdom and of understanding, the Spirit of counsel and of might,the Spirit of the knowledge and fear of the LORD—* ***3*** *and he will delight in the fear of the LORD. He will not judge by what he sees with his eyes, or decide by what he hears with his ears;* ***4*** *but with righteousness he will judge the needy, with justice he will give decisions for the poor of the earth. He will strike the earth with the rod of his mouth; with the breath of his lips he will slay the wicked.* ***5*** *Righteousness will be his belt and faithfulness the sash around his waist.* ***6*** *The wolf will live with the lamb,the leopard will lie down with the goat, the calf and the lion and the yearling together; and a little child will lead them.* ***7*** *The cow will feed with the bear, their young will lie down together, and the lion will eat straw like the ox.* ***8*** *The infant will play near the cobra's den, and the young child will put its hand into the viper's nest. They will neither harm nor destroy on all my holy mountain, for the*

> *earth will be filled with the knowledge of the LORD*
> *as the waters cover the sea.* (Isaiah 11:1–9 NIV)

This passage is mostly about the future Kingdom of God under the rule of the Messiah (Christ). In verse 4, we are told he will judge according to what is right in God's eyes. Thus, the poor will be given justice. In most legal systems in our world (as in most economic and political systems), the poor are not as likely to get justice. There are great advantages to having money, such as being able to hire a good lawyer or to hire lobbyists to advocate for your cause. The result is that the poor do not often get justice in any area of life. But, in the Kingdom of God, all get justice. That reinforces the idea that we should be working for justice for all—judicial, social, and economic justice.

In verses 6–9, we see a wonderful picture of the animals living together in peace. Predators do not harm other animals or human beings. This makes clear that the way things are in our world, is not the way God intended it to be. However, it seems likely that we will not be able to reverse these things—it will take an act of God to do it, and I doubt we can even bring in the beginnings of it now. There are some aspects of the future Kingdom that will simply have to wait for the future!

However, in verse 9, there is something we can be working on now: "The earth will be full of the knowledge of the Lord." How can we bring that about in its beginnings now? We can start by getting to know the Lord more deeply through the spiritual disciplines. We can spend time studying the Word of God, both alone and with others. Sermons and group Bible studies can be helpful. We can also learn to *meditate on the Word* on our own. That can simply mean reflecting deeply on Scripture. Or, it can mean using our imagination to enter into the stories of the Bible.

Prayer can also be a way to get to know God more deeply. Christians long ago referred to *prayer* as "keeping company with God." When we fellowship with God, we get to know him. There are many resources available on Christian spirituality through groups like Renovare.

Of course, we are also called to spread our knowledge of the Lord to others—to spread the Gospel, and to teach people to live by the teachings of Jesus.

> 1 *In the last days the mountain of the LORD's temple will be established as the highest of the mountains; it will be exalted above the hills, and peoples will stream to it. Many nations will come and say, Come, let us go up to the mountain of the LORD, to the temple of the God of Jacob. He will teach us his ways, so that we may walk in his paths." The law will go out from Zion, the word of the LORD from Jerusalem. He will judge between many peoples and will settle disputes for strong nations far and wide. They will beat their swords into plowshares and their spears into pruning hooks. Nation will not take up sword against nation, nor will they train for war anymore. Everyone will sit under their own vine and under their own fig tree, and no one will make them afraid, for the LORD Almighty has spoken.* (Micah 4:1–4 NIV)

In verse 3, we see that nations will "beat their swords into plowshares," and not go to war anymore. Is this really possible in our current situation? Given the sinfulness of humanity, it seems unlikely that war will be abolished anytime soon! But what this passage suggests to us as Christians is that we can work for peace, and advocate for it. Christians in the "peace churches" have suggested that if we worked as hard for peace as we do to prepare for war, there might be more peace and less war. That's likely true.

****

> 9 *After this I looked, and there before me was a great multitude that no one could count, from every nation, tribe, people and language, standing before the throne and before the Lamb. They were wearing white robes and were holding palm branches in their hands.* 10 *And they cried out in a loud voice: "Salvation belongs to our God, who sits on the throne, and to the Lamb."*
> 11 *All the angels were standing around the throne and around the elders and the four living creatures. They fell down on their faces before the throne and worshiped God, saying:*
> 12 *"Amen! Praise and glory and wisdom and thanks and honor and power and strength be to our God forever and ever. Amen!" (Revelation 7:9-12)*

This is, I believe, a picture of the future Kingdom. Believers are together, worshiping God and "the lamb" (Jesus). The most obvious application is that we as believers should get together and worship the Lord.

What may be a little less obvious is that these people that constitute the future Kingdom are from "every nation, tribe, people, and language." We are going to share heaven and the new earth with all kinds of people—of different ethnic, racial, national, and cultural backgrounds. And the universal church of our day is also similarly diverse.

One implication for us today is this: It affects how we see ourselves and our first loyalty. In Philippians 3:20, Paul reminds us that "our citizenship is in heaven." To put it another way, our citizenship is first and foremost in the Kingdom of God. Is it possible that many Christians see themselves as being firstly citizens of the nation they live in? Do they see that as their first loyalty? But I would remind them that is only temporary. We will be citizens of God's Kingdom for all eternity! Likewise, the values of every human culture is a mixed bag of both good and evil, but the values of the Kingdom are totally good and righteous.

A second implication is this: If we are going to spend eternity with all these different people— and worship God together with them—why not get started on that here and now? Some have presented a compelling argument for multiethnic congregations based at least partly on this passage. There are many diverse communities in the United States where multiethnic congregations would be a great witness to the world. In a world full of divisions and hate, it would show that we as Christians can worship, fellowship, and work together in Christian love.

****

> 4 *He will wipe every tear from their eyes. There will be no more death or mourning or crying or pain, for the old order of things has passed away.* (Revelation 21:4 NIV)

This is a picture of the new creation. Heaven has come down to the new earth, where God's people will live in full fellowship with God. There will be no sorrow, death, or pain, we are told.

These things are all a result of sin. Since sin is gone—banished from the new creation—so are all the curses. We will be free to live the life that God originally intended for us before sin entered the scene.

What might bringing in the beginnings of that look like? We can battle against unnecessary pain and sickness and sorrow. That might suggest ministries of compassion for the hurting. It might also imply finding ways to give everyone access to good healthcare. We can seek to prevent premature deaths. One church in an urban neighborhood with a high rate of violent crime has been working to teach teenagers how to resolve conflict in nonviolent ways. Dozens of teens have been mentored in these Christian methods of conflict resolution. These are just a few possibilities. The fact is, Christian faith changes lives (and societies) where it is taken seriously.

6. In light of our future hope, we are called to pursue God's big agenda in our lives, rather than our selfish little agendas.

> 17 *Therefore, if anyone is in Christ, the new creation has come: The old has gone, the new is here!* 18 *All this is from God, who reconciled us to himself through Christ and gave us the ministry of reconciliation:* 19 *that God was reconciling the world to himself in Christ, not counting people's sins against them. And he has committed to us the message of reconciliation.* 20 *We are therefore Christ's ambassadors, as though God were making his appeal through us. We implore you on Christ's behalf: Be reconciled to God.* 21 *God made him who had no sin to be sin for us, so that in him we might become the righteousness of God.* (2 Corinthians 5:17–21 NIV)

Most of us humans have our own little agenda for our life. It may include such things as making a lot of money, being successful in the eyes of the world, having a nice family and some good friends, being recognized and admired, having good health and a long life, and having some fun along the way. These kinds of things are not necessarily bad, but they do not produce real meaning or joy in life, either. What we need is to plug into a cause greater than ourselves and give ourselves to it.

What greater cause is there than to plug into God's big agenda for the world? It is the great plan for God to redeem a fallen humanity and restore us to paradise. It is to create a new humanity, forgiven and reconciled to him, who joyfully accept God's reign, and trust God to bring about a new creation.

"If anyone is in Christ, he is a new creation." God created the first humans in his image, but they went bad. So now he is creating a new humanity. In Christ, he is reconciling people to himself. He is granting us forgiveness and a new start. He is restoring the image of God in us. And he has commissioned us to be his ambassadors.

What does it mean to be an ambassador? Every nation in our world sends ambassadors to other nations. These persons are citizens of their home country. They are sent to foreign countries to represent their homeland and live out its culture and values. They speak forth messages from the leaders of their own land. As Christians, we are citizens of the Kingdom of God. We live in a foreign land but live by the values of our homeland. And we speak for our own country and its leader—Jesus. We are to call people to be reconciled to God, and to enter his Kingdom and be part of the new humanity that accepts God's reign in their lives.

We need to commit ourselves to building our life around God's agenda. Too often, Christians build their life around their own agenda. We may think being a Christian means living a moral life and being a nice person—all the while pursuing our own selfish agenda.

That would suggest that all we need to do is not make the world any worse. But, the reality is, the world is broken. People are desperately hurting. They are not in fellowship with God. Their lives are not whole. The reality of death looms over them. It is not enough to avoid making the world worse. We need to make it better. We need to become God's agents in creating a new humanity that will someday live in a restored paradise. By the power of the Holy Spirit living in us, we can continue the ministry of Jesus, and thus offer real change and real hope. That is our calling!

STUDY GUIDE

RESPOND IN FAITH

1. JOHN 3:16—What does it mean to believe in him? Is it more than agreeing with certain doctrines?
2. What else is involved?
3. MARK 1:14–15—What is the Kingdom of God? What does it mean to repent?
4. EPHESIANS 2:8–9—Is there any way we can earn our own salvation? Does our faith earn us salvation?

HOPE FOR THE FUTURE

1. HEBREWS 2:14–15—How did Jesus free us from enslavement to the fear of death?

DOWNHILL OR BEST YET TO COME?

1. 2 CORINTHIANS 4:16–18—Why might it be easy for older people to "lose heart?" What kind of losses might they be dealing with? Why does Paul say he does not lose heart?

BEING READY FOR THE SECOND COMING

1. MATTHEW 25:14–30—What is the basis for judgment in this parable?
2. MATTHEW 25:31–46—When does this scene take place? What is the basis for judgment here? Does this contradict the truth that salvation is by grace through faith?
3. 1 JOHN 3:2–3—How does this passage suggest we prepare for Christ's Second Coming?
4. 2 PETER 3:11—In light of the Second Coming, what kind of people should we be?

5. MATTHEW 24:14—How does this verse imply we may speed the coming of Jesus?

IMPLICATIONS OF DESCRIPTIONS OF THE FUTURE KINGDOM

1. ISAIAH 11:1–9—Who is being spoken of here? When will he act as judge? Who will he give justice to? What might this suggest we can be working toward now? "The earth will be full of the knowledge of the Lord"—how can we work toward that now?
2. MICAH 4:1–4—Since there will be no more war in the future Kingdom of God, what might that suggest we should work toward here and now?
3. REVELATION 7:9–12—Who are these people? Given the great diversity of this crowd, does this suggest some things we could be working toward now?
4. REVELATION 21:4—Where and when will this be true? What implications might this have for our ministry now?

GOD'S AGENDA VERSUS OURS

1. 2 CORINTHIANS 5:17–21—What kind of personal agenda do most people have? What does it consist of?
   a. What is God's big agenda, as revealed in this passage? What is an *ambassador*?
   b. Many people think the Christian life just involves "being moral" and "being nice," while pursuing our own agenda. Why is this not enough?

CHAPTER 6

PULLING IT ALL TOGETHER

When we are young, most of us deal with death by assuming it is something that just happens to old people. That was my general approach. It served me well until I was eleven years old, and a friend my age drowned in a local lake. But then, I got to thinking about it, and how Tommy was always doing stupid dangerous stuff, so that's why he died. So, that got me back to thinking that death usually just happens to old people. Then, add in the fact that I have never seen myself as an old person, and this translates to "death happens to other people."

That idea took a big hit when my parents died, and I realized my generation was next in line. Years later, I hit sixty-five. My heart said I was still young, but my head knew I was getting old. A few more years, and a trip to the hospital with heart problems, and it started to sink in. Death could be right around the corner. Then, add in the COVID-19 pandemic in 2020, with people all around me dying, and I had to face my own mortality.

So, where did this thing called *death* come from? And what kind of afterlife is there to look forward to? As a pastor, I had preached about this many times, especially at funerals. But I had never done a thorough systematic study of what the Bible has to say about it. Given that everything was shut down during the pandemic, what a great opportunity to do that study!

The story begins near the beginning of Genesis, with God creating this beautiful garden paradise and placing the first humans (Adam and Eve) in it. They had ideal living conditions, creative work to do, and the opportunity to relate to God face-to-face. Their relationship to each other and to the rest of creation was also idyllic.

But there was also an evil force in the garden, which tempted them to distrust and disobey God. They fell for it, and sin thus entered the world. God pronounced curses on them and their world, and they were thrown out of the garden. Ever since then, humans have all been broken people in a broken world. Life is not what it was intended to be. Relationships are damaged (most especially our relationship to God). Work is frustrating. Nature is cursed.

Worst of all, death entered the world. With it came great fear and pain and sorrow. It brought separation from loved ones. Bereavement is one of the greatest sorrows in life. How we miss our departed loved ones! How we long to be with them again!

With death also came violence, as humans realized they could inflict death on each other. As time went on, the world was so filled with wickedness and violence, that the Lord was sorry he made humans (see Genesis 6:6).

But, instead of giving up on us, God initiated a long-range plan to redeem us and to restore paradise. It is a plan that addresses what is wrong with our world (and with the human race) and, ultimately, sets it right. It also gives us a purpose for our life now that is connected with God's wonderful future for us. And it is comforting to know that life on earth is going somewhere good, according to God's wise plan. It is not just random events going nowhere, ending in the grave. It is not just a meaningless mess.

Central to God's plan is the sending of his Son Jesus to live among us as one of us. God did not remove all the suffering and death from the world but, in Christ, got in there and suffered with us. He lived a human life, experiencing the same types of things we experience. Jesus understands all the ways that life is hard and intercedes for us with God the Father. He experienced the pain and sorrow of bereavement when his earthly father died. And, ultimately, he experienced his own death, which was not only a way of identifying with us, but also to atone for our sins.

But Jesus Christ did not remain dead—God raised him from the dead. As the hymn "Christ Arose" by Robert Lowry puts it:

> *Death could not keep his prey, Jesus my Savior,*
> *He tore the bars away, Jesus my Lord.*
> *Up from the grave he arose, with a mighty triumph*
> *o'er his foes . . . ."*

Jesus rose from the dead, but it was not like the raising of Lazarus, who came back to the same body and then died again sometime later. Jesus rose to a new body with different physical properties. So he could appear to his disciples, and could even go through closed doors. The disciples wondered if they were seeing a ghost. But he showed them he could eat food and could be touched. His body was definitely physical. Was it really him? He showed them the marks from the nails in his hands and feet. And some of the things he said—and, perhaps, the way he said them—made it clear this was the same person. It was Jesus in his "glorified" body. It was a body that could never die again.

The resurrection of Jesus has been seen as a kind of vindication of him as the Messiah and the Son of God. Thus, it assures us that he really could and did die for our sins. It validates his message and his atonement. He paid for our sins. We can be forgiven!

However, his resurrection means more than that. Our whole hope of an afterlife is based upon it. He was the "firstfruits," the beginning of the harvest that points to the rest of the harvest.

We as his followers will be the rest of the harvest. Our resurrection will occur when Jesus comes again. Our resurrection is inseparable from that of Jesus; they are two parts of one event. So, it is like God brought a person from the future into the present. Jesus thus showed us our future and paved the way for it.

We will be raised to a body like the glorified body of Jesus. We will each have a new improved body, but it will still be us. There will be continuity of identity. Yet we will be in a form that is well- suited for the new life. It will not be subject to disease, pain, decay, and death. And we will no longer sin—we will be free of that. The image of God will be fully restored in us. We will thus be able to become what God intended us to be from the start.

Some Christians have the idea that after we die, we will simply go to heaven and happily live there forever as disembodied souls. This is an idea that comes from the teachings of Plato, an ancient Greek philosopher. He believed that the body is like a prison house, and that we should be glad to be rid of it. That is understandable, since our present bodies have so many limitations and weaknesses.

But that is not the teaching of the Bible. We were made for bodily life, and God has promised to replace our weak mortal bodies with glorious immortal ones.

The reality of the resurrection of Jesus—with all that it implies and points toward—was central to the preaching of the apostles in the Book of Acts. It is a life-changing truth that informs and empowers our life today and gives us a great hope for the future. It changed the early disciples from a group of despairing, defeated, and hopeless persons, to a bunch of joyous, hope-filled, and unstoppable followers of Jesus. And, yes, they conquered the Roman Empire without ever killing anyone! They risked their lives—and many gave their lives—for the cause of Christ, because they believed in the resurrection of the dead.

That resurrection will occur when Jesus comes again. But that is only part of what will happen then. A whole new world will be created then. All of the current creation groans under the curse—it is chaotic, polluted, messed up, and dangerous. It needs to be set right. God will create a new heaven and a new earth that will include the beautiful things of our current earth, but not the bad. Does that mean the present earth will be renovated, cleaned up, and restored? Or will God completely destroy it, and then create a whole new world from scratch? Some passages of Scripture suggest renewal, others a whole new beginning.

The real point is that our whole world needs to be redeemed. What good would it do to put redeemed people onto a cursed and broken earth? The curse of sin goes beyond human individuals. So must the redemption. It must extend to human systems and institutions, which will need to be cleaned up. (Did you ever notice that whoever has been voted into political power, things are still a mess?)

Beyond that, the earth itself is a mess. Think about it: floods, droughts, famines, earthquakes, destructive storms, heat waves, cold spells, and so much more. The physical world needs to be redeemed! And it will be! All this will happen when Jesus comes again, and the world as we know it is brought to an end.

But there's yet more to happen when Jesus comes again. People who have not renounced evil cannot be allowed into this new creation and its new society—or they will destroy it. So there must be a decisive battle with the forces of evil, and then there must be a final judgment.

The same Jesus who came as a suffering servant, to seek and to save the lost, will at his Second Coming be a conqueror who defeats the forces of evil. Those who insist on resisting God must be defeated.

Then there must be a judgment. All humans will have to stand before the throne of God to be judged according to what they did on earth in their life. Those whose names are written in the Book of Life (which would be those who turned to the Lord in repentant faith) are acquitted. They go to be with the Lord on the new earth. The others (who have not renounced evil) must be separated out and sent to another place.

Those people who have trusted in God get to enter into the fullness of fellowship with Him. This is the highlight of the new world—we get to see God face-to-face and have perfect fellowship with him. We were made for fellowship with God, so what could be better? And, as we get to know God more deeply, worship will be our natural response.

But there will also be much more to do on this new earth. We are told that we will serve him and reign with him forever. That suggests we will have work to do. Thank God! As I have thought about the afterlife, I have found that one of my great fears is that I will be bored. I mean, there will be a lot of time, so we better have plenty to do! As a retired person, I have often had lots of time on my hands. Though I try to keep busy doing the Lord's work (as a volunteer), there have been times when I have been bored. And I have not enjoyed that. So, an eternity with nothing to do sounds awful!

Scripture tells us that God worked in creating this world—and is still at work in our world. There was also work for Adam and Eve to do before sin entered the world. Part of being made in God's image is that we need creative work to do.

There are many more details about the new creation, especially in the Book of Revelation. There are two of them that are especially worthy of our attention. Revelation 22 speaks of "the river of the water of life" that flows from the throne of God. This life-giving water will be available to all of us on the new earth. It will also water the tree of life, the fruit of which bestows everlasting life. That is the tree that Adam and Eve were denied access to, after they had sinned against God. If they had eaten of it, they would have lived forever. In a world full of evil, living forever might have been disastrous and miserable. But on the new earth, where there is no sin, living forever would be a joy and a delight.

Many other details of the new earth are given to us, but I suspect most of them are better discerned with the right brain than the left. In the Western world, we want to approach everything with logic and analysis. But I believe much of Scripture is best approached with our imagination and intuition. Maybe that's why so much of Scripture is stories or poetry or metaphor, rather than propositional truth. Much of what the writer of Revelation saw was simply beyond his ability to describe to us. He probably did not really understand it all himself, so he simply drew us some pictures with words. We might do well to just imagine it, feel it, and experience it. And then to give thanks to God for our indescribably wonderful future!

Our ultimate destiny is living in a resurrection body in this great new world that will be brought in when Jesus comes again. When will that be? No one but God the Father knows the hour. We do know it has already been nearly 2,000 years since Christ's prophecies of his Second Coming. So what has happened to Christians who have died during that time? And what will happen to us if we die before he comes again?

The Bible does speak to these questions, though not in great detail. It seems quite clear that upon death, God's people immediately go to a blessed place. It is referred to in Scripture in various ways: *paradise, heaven, Abraham's bosom,* and other ways. Sometimes, we say, "My loved one went to be with the Lord."

That itself may be the greatest thing about this place. Paul describes it this way: "Away from the body . . . at home with the Lord" (2 Corinthians 5:8). And he makes it clear that this is better than life on this earth. But he also makes it clear that he looks forward to the day of resurrection, and the new creation. That is our ultimate salvation.

So, we could say that our salvation comes in three steps. Christians experience something of the abundant life here on this earth after we put our faith in Jesus. We start to have restored fellowship with God. We enjoy the loving fellowship between fellow believers. And, life generally goes better as we grow in our obedience to the Lord,

If we die before Jesus comes again, we enjoy step 2. We go to be with the Lord in a beautiful garden paradise. We are fully conscious. And we are reunited with our departed loved ones. This is very good, but still not the ultimate blessing God has in store for us.

When Jesus comes again, we enter step 3: resurrection of the body, the new creation, and more. This is our full salvation and full restoration. God restores us as individuals, as well as the whole creation. God sets things right and sets up his reign of righteousness. Wouldn't you just love to see everything be totally right and good? Jesus for President!

The overall picture of our blessed future is absolutely great! But the details of the new creation are not always clear. And the details of "heaven" (step 2) are rather sketchy.

Recently, my wife and I traveled to Bermuda to see our daughter (who has been living there for work reasons for several months). We have had many phone conversations with her during these months. She has verbally described so many wonderful things about this strange island in the middle of the Atlantic Ocean. She has also sent us pictures. So we have been trying to imagine this beautiful place. But when we got there, it was much different than what we had imagined.

I thought about this, and it occurred to me how much more this would be true of heaven and the new earth. We have some glowing descriptions of each place and of the afterlife, enough to make us feel really good about it. We have every reason to trust God for his plans for us. But when we get there, it seems quite certain that things will be very different from what we have imagined. They will probably be much better! People who thought they had it all figured out, will just shake their heads and laugh. But because it's better, who can complain?

So, the point is, embrace the overall picture, and trust God to fill in the details!

OUR RESPONSE

We have seen the human problem (sin and death) and God's solution (redemption and new life). So, what does it mean for our life here and now? What is to be our response? First of all, we need to be ready for the Second Coming and all it will usher in: resurrection, judgment, new creation, and more.

Only those whose name is written in the Book of Life will get to enjoy the great future God has prepared for his people. We need to experience the spiritual birth Jesus speaks of in John chapter 3. We need to repent and believe in Jesus. Then, we will be part of the family of God who are heirs of the promises of future blessings. Then, we will be among those who have been given "new birth into a living hope through the resurrection of Jesus Christ from the dead, and into an inheritance that can never perish, spoil, or fade" (1 Peter 1:3–4).

Second, as God's people, we have been called to *get ready* (or be prepared for) the Second Coming. We don't want to be caught sleeping or living wrongly when Jesus appears. But what if you just happen to be sleeping when he comes? Or watching a ballgame on TV? Or having a fight with your spouse? No problem. The point is, "What is the whole pattern of your life?" Is it one that reflects saving faith?

Virtually, every New Testament passage on the Second Coming is directly linked with a call to godly living, faithful service, or spiritual growth. Some people get so caught up in speculative theology and intricate details about the Second Coming that they completely miss the crucial life—applications in Scripture.

There are people who think they are "prophecy experts." They may even write books telling us which current world leader is the anti-Christ of end times, or what countries will fight Israel in the final battle. Many years ago, some said that Hitler was the anti-Christ. They were proven wrong. Indeed, there has been quite a history of getting it wrong when it comes to unclear details of biblical prophecy. All the way back in the first century, there were "prophecy experts" among God's people who decided that Jesus could not be the Messiah, because he did not fit their interpretations of certain Old Testament passages. They got it wrong in a big way!

It may be that we would do well to avoid books that major in unclear prophetic passages or intricate theology of the end times. They may seem interesting, but the Bible is not there for our amusement. It is not a crystal ball or a horoscope or a palm reader. Remember that "history of getting it wrong." And be humble about interpreting prophetic passages that are not at all clear, or are not reinforced by other biblical passages.

What would be the basic pattern of your life if Jesus came again today (or if you died today)? Would you be found spending much time on idle speculation or controversies on minor theological points about the end times? Are you obsessed with making a lot of money? Do you waste your whole life on entertainment? Are you a news junkie or a sports junkie? How about video games? Are you addicted to porn or drugs or gambling? Some of these things are harmful in and of themselves and some are not. But do you want to be found centering your life around them?

Based on the teachings of Jesus, our lives should be centered on Christian service, giving to the poor and to Christian ministries, growing our spiritual life, and doing our daily work (job) as unto the Lord. If these are not your priorities, you may want to make some changes—before it's too late. When Jesus comes again, we will all be held accountable.

There is a related point that needs to be made. All of us have our own little selfish agenda in life. It comes natural. It may include getting rich, being successful in the eyes of the world, being admired, and having some fun along the way. These things may not be bad, but neither do they produce real joy or meaning in life. Many people think that *being a Christian* means living a decent moral life and being a nice person, all while pursuing our own selfish agenda. They have missed the point, and they may find their lives empty and depressing.

What we need is to plug into a cause that is greater than ourselves. The Kingdom of God is the greatest cause of all. In other words, we need to continue the ministry of Jesus. We need to work for positive change in ourselves, in others, and in our world.

How do we go about that? There is plenty of guidance in Scripture, especially in the teachings of Jesus. But we can also get some help from biblical pictures of the future Kingdom, which may show us what God's perfect will is for the world.

Isaiah loves to talk about justice for the poor and the oppressed, even in messianic passages. In the future Kingdom of God, the Messiah will rule with perfect justice for the poor. So, it makes sense that we should work for justice in our society.

We are also called to work for peace. War is a terrible thing. Even career military persons will tell you so. Wherever there is an incredible humanitarian disaster in the world, you can bet it was created by war. Some Christians are pacifists, and some are not. Yet we can all agree that war is a terrible thing. We can all work for and advocate for peace. We will not be able to prevent all warfare, but maybe we can prevent some wars.

We can also work for reconciliation between people of different racial/ethnic/cultural groups. Look at the picture in Revelation 7—people from "every nation, tribe, people, and language." That's who would make up the future Kingdom of God. In heaven, and later on the new earth, that's who we are going to spend eternity with. And the universal church today is similarly diverse. In fact, the greatest growth in the Church is in places like Africa, Latin America, India, and China.

Have you ever had fellowship with Christians from some of these places? I have had wonderful fellowship with Christians from Nigeria. They have been through some great suffering, which has brought them closer to God. Many of them are godly people, and true prayer warriors. I also remember Ethiopian refugees, who had come to the Lord through some extreme trials. They formed a church here in the United States, and "nested" in the church facilities of a church I pastored. They are delightful people, and full of the Holy Spirit. I have been blessed with knowing beautiful Christians from the Dominican Republic, India, China, Korea, and other places. I have found I have more in common with them than I do with white nominal Christians in the United States.

When my wife and I lived near Harrisburg, PA, we attended a church that was about half African American and half white. It was a great thing to fellowship with people of different races and cultures. We live in a society that has too much hate and division. When you worship with—and get to know—people of different races and cultures, you get to understand and love them. As Christians, we can be the answer to the hate and division in our society and our world.

There are other pictures of the future Kingdom that may suggest possible ministries for us to support financially and/or be involved in: ministries of compassion, ministries to draw people into deeper fellowship with God, and evangelistic efforts to invite people to faith in Christ.

Finally, there is one more important response we can make to God's solution to our human problem. It has to do with the way we look at life. It may be summed up with the word *hope.* Many modern philosophers and novelists have come to believe that death is the end of us. As a result, they have come to see life as totally meaningless and hopeless. Whether you are rich or poor, live a good life or a bad life, none of it matters. In the end, you wind up dead and gone. Everything is futile.

Not only that, but we spend our life in fear of death. And that is a kind of slavery, Hebrews 2:15 tells us. Look at the freedom the apostles had because of the resurrection of Jesus. Their enemies threatened to kill them if they did not stop preaching the Gospel. Did they cringe in fear? Did they give up? No, they were willing to risk death. Because they believed there was life beyond death. Because Jesus had risen from the dead. Because they knew by faith that they would be raised from the dead to a glorified body like that of Jesus and would live with him forever. Because they knew the future life (afterlife) would be much better than life here. Because they believed the promises of God. Faith in God's promises regarding the afterlife is liberating! It casts a whole new light on life here and now!

In our nation today, many elderly people suffer from depression. As we get older, our bodies fall apart. We experience pain and sickness. A woman in one of the churches I pastored said it well: "When it comes to my body, anything that don't hurt, it don't work." That speaks to the aches and pains. It points to the fact that parts of our body may not work very well anymore. Things we took for granted when we were young are now diminished or gone. And it's all part of the aging process.

It's all about losses. I live in an active senior community and, sometimes, when we get together we talk about this. My eyesight isn't what it used to be, one says. Another is not quite as mobile. Another has to use a hearing aid because her hearing is not so great now. A man struggles with terrible pain in his back. A friend jokes about being a bionic man because he has had knee replacements on both knees plus a hip replacement. And we all take medications for our heart and/or something else.

Then, there are the emotional losses. A significant percentage of the people in our 9,000-person community are widowed.

Most have lost a close friend. All of us have lost most of the things we enjoy during the pandemic. Almost everything has been shut down.

Losses and more losses, followed by death. Is that all we have to look forward to? Many seniors are asking themselves, "Is it all downhill from here?" The apostle Paul speaks to this in 2 Corinthians 4:16–18. He speaks of outwardly wasting away. But he points out that he is inwardly being renewed day by day. And he speaks of the hope of eternal glory in his future.

There is hope for us as Christian seniors on many levels. First of all, we can be growing in Christ (being inwardly renewed) till the day we die. We should never stop growing spiritually. The hardships we face can help deepen our relationship to the Lord.

Second, we can keep doing Christian service. We have more time and lots of life experience. "Always give yourself fully to the work of the Lord, because you know that your labor in the Lord is not in vain." (1 Corinthians 15:58) It is not wasted because, in the end, God and goodness will triumph. We are on the winning side. We know this because Jesus rose from the dead.

Third, once we do come to the end of our life on earth, we have the glorious hope of an afterlife that is better than our life on earth. The best is yet to come! We can look forward to life in fellowship with God—first in paradise and, later on, the new earth. We don't know all the details, but we can trust God to give us everything we need.

That does not mean we should become escapist in our thinking. It's easy to feel as if the world is totally hopeless, so we'll just sit around waiting for the Second Coming or death, so we can just escape it all. Too many Christians have become pessimistic and despairing and hopeless about our world. But, remember, God is still at work in our world. So, things can change. No person—or society—is beyond redemption.

More persons than ever are coming to faith in Christ every day. More wonderful Christian ministries of compassion and evangelism are being born. More hungry people are being fed. God is still at work in our world. So, there is always the possibility of spiritual renewal, or of gradual positive changes.

Our calling is to continue the work of Jesus, by the power of the Holy Spirit, which is tapped by prayer. When the time is right, Jesus will come again. And God will set all things right. And we will receive the fullness of our salvation.

No, it is not all downhill from here. We are not a people of fear and despair. We are a people of hope! THE BEST IS YET TO COME!

STUDY GUIDE

1. Where did death come from? When did it enter the world? Is it a good thing or a bad thing?
2. What other curses came into the world along with death?
3. Does God have a redemptive plan for us and our world? Why did God send his son into the world?
4. What is the significance of the resurrection of Jesus? What does the term *firstfruits* imply?
5. What events will happen when Jesus comes again?
6. Where will believers spend eternity? What do you think will be the highlight of this new world? Will there be work for us to do?
7. Where have we previously read about the tree of life? What blessing does it bestow?
8. What happens to Christians who die before Jesus comes again? Is this better than life here and now?
9. According to this book, what are the three steps of our salvation?

OUR RESPONSE

1. How can we make sure we are ready for Jesus to come again?
2. How is God's agenda different from the typical selfish agenda of most people?
3. How do descriptions of the future Kingdom of God (in Scripture) help inform us as to what we are to be doing now? Give some specific examples.
4. Why might senior citizens lose hope and feel depressed? What are three ways our faith can give us hope as we age?
5. Do you ever feel that our world is on a hopeless downhill slide? Are there any people—or nations—that are beyond redemption? How is God still at work in our world? What are some of the great things God is doing through his people? When you think of these things, does that give you hope?

EPILOGUE

After I wrote the text of this book, three persons I loved died within a month's time. They were all people my wife and I were close to at one time. First, there was David, who played piano in a church I pastored. He was a kind and gracious Christian man, and a musician whose excellent skills enhanced our worship.

Not long after, we lost Jim, a member of our Life Group and our men's group in the church we currently attend. Following his retirement, he gave himself to faithful service to the church. He was recently diagnosed with stage 4 cancer. The last time I saw him in the hospital, he told me that none of the treatments were working, and the cancer was spreading rapidly. He said that he expected to die soon, and that this was kind of scary. He was glad I had written this book and shared it with the men's group. For him, it had been a timely reminder of our hope in Christ. That was the last time I saw him.

A couple of weeks later, Joanna died. She and her husband had been in our small group in another church I pastored. She was an exemplary Christian woman. We loved her and were so sad to hear of her passing.

When I thought about these precious friends dying, I remembered what my mother said to me when she was getting older: “One of the hardest things about growing old is that my best friends are all dead.” I was also reminded of the pain of separation from loved ones that comes with death.

But we also have a wonderful hope in Christ. All of them died with that hope for a “better country” (see Hebrews 12:16).

In writing this book, I have been comforted by our hope as put forth in God’s Word. I have also been challenged to be faithful in service for the Kingdom. My wish is that you have been blessed in reading it. My prayer is that many more people will be helped by it.

APPENDIX A

A PRAYER TO PRAY WHEN FACING DEATH

Heavenly Father,

More than ever, I know that I am not in control of my life, and it's scary. Strengthen my faith, as I face death, the ultimate test of my faith. Help me to trust wholly in you.

Have mercy in relation to the physical pain. And there is such emotional pain, too, as I will soon have to leave the people I love. Help me to let go and help them in their grieving.

Thank you for your love and grace. Thank you for the hope we have in Christ. I look forward to seeing you and my departed Christian loved ones in the wonderful place you have prepared for us. I look forward to a new world in which everything is set right, and there is no more sin, suffering, and death.

O Lord, I desperately need your presence now more than ever. Bring me safely through to the other side.

In Jesus' name I pray, Amen.

A PRAYER IN THE HYMN: GUIDE ME, O THOU GREAT JEHOVAH

by William Williams, 1745

When I tread the verge of Jordan,
Bid my anxious fears subside.
Death of death and hell's destruction,
Land me safe on Canaan's side.
Songs of praises, songs of praises,
I will ever give to thee,
I will ever give to thee.

APPENDIX B

STATEMENTS ON THE AFTERLIFE IN HISTORIC CREEDS

APOSTLES CREED—"I believe in . . . the resurrection of the body; and the life everlasting."

NICENE CREED—"We look for the resurrection of the dead, and the life of the world to come."

WESTMINSTER CONFESSION OF FAITH, CHAPTER 32—"The bodies of men, after death, return to dust, and see corruption; but their souls (which neither die nor sleep), having an immortal subsistence, immediately return to God who gave them. The souls of the righteous, being then made perfect in holiness, are received into the highest heavens, where they behold the face of God in light and glory, waiting for the full redemption of their bodies."

THE HEIDELBERG CATECHISM, QUESTION 45—"What benefit do we receive from the resurrection of Christ? Answer—First, by his resurrection, he has overcome death that he might make us share in the righteousness which he has obtained for us through his death. Second, we too are now raised by his power to a new life. Third, the resurrection of Christ is a sure pledge to us of our blessed resurrection."

NOTE: These confessions are quoted from the BOOK OF CONFESSIONS OF THE PRESBYTERIAN CHURCH (USA)

CPSIA information can be obtained
at www.ICGtesting.com
Printed in the USA
BVHW031215110722
641843BV00012B/606